The Global Baseball Classroom

About the Author

Brent Loehr is a teacher, coach, and writer from Western Canada. He earned a baseball scholarship as a catcher out of high school and later graduated with a Bachelor of Education (English, Physical Education, and Coaching). In his late twenties, Brent travelled the globe for Major League Baseball International spreading the game overseas. After starting a family, he went on hiatus from these trips and focused on another interest that would keep him closer to home: writing. Brent earned a Diploma in Writing from St. Peter's College and later a spot in the Saskatchewan Writers' Guild mentorship program. Brent's work has appeared in *Prairies North, Swedish Press, WestWorld, The Society, TRANSITION, Going Places, Canadian Musician,* and *The Canadian Baseball Network. The Global Baseball Classroom* is his first book.

The Global Baseball Classroom

Brent Loehr

SUMMER
GAME
BOOKS

Published by Summer Game Books

ISBN: 978-1-938545-62-7 (print)
ISBN: 978-1-938545-63-4 (ebook)

For information about permissions, bulk purchases, or additional distribution, write to

Summer Game Books
P. O. Box 818
South Orange, NJ 07079
or contact the publisher at
www.summergamebooks.com

If you have ever dreamed of travels to far-off locales – or have been captivated by the possibilities of a white ball with red seams – or simply read for pleasure and not judgement - I ask you, with more gratitude than I can express, to split the dedication of this book in equal parts between my parents, wife, and family.

In memory of my father, Mervin Loehr, whom I wish could have had the chance to read this book.

Contents

The Global Baseball Classroom

A wrap-up game to end a session of skill work in Uganda.

Introduction

"You spend a good piece of your life gripping a baseball and in the end it turns out that it was the other way around all the time."

—Jim Bouton

Baseball has been a constant in my life, affording friendships and memories that will last until Alzheimer's eventually smears them. My dad aside, the game has been one of my greatest teachers. It has also brought forth many fortuitous events. The boundaries of Saskatchewan capably confined me like a hitter in the batter's box while growing up. Baseball, my passion, later became a vehicle for another interest—travel. Little did I know that the two combined would eventually lead to stories from across the globe that I simply couldn't concoct—and often lessons learned from remarkable people, places, and circumstances.

I played all of my youth baseball in my hometown of Muenster, Saskatchewan, just like generations of family before me. In the local tavern hangs a team picture from the early 1900s—including my great-great grandfather's sons who had come up from Minnesota prior. After graduating high school in 1993 I earned a scholarship as a catcher. I often drove Coach David Richter nuts continually pestering him to dip our bus across state borders so I could 'experience' another part of America. In my senior year, after returning home that summer, I blew out my shoulder at 22 years old in a tournament in British Columbia. It required surgery.

To say I was depressed is an understatement. I soon began my career as a teacher back in Central Sasketchewan, and still

An outline of the day's activities for the MLB Roadshow held at Wiesbaden, Germany.

wanting to remain in the game at an advanced level, began coaching baseball more formally. I became involved in the National Coaching Certification Program in Canada and coached with Saskatchewan Baseball's elite all-star programs. I sought out and completed every coaching course I could find. During a clinic I noticed a poster on a wall: *The harder you work, the luckier you get.* I worked.

I became more competent. I became certified as a facilitator to train up-and-coming coaches. My 'luck' started to come when my preparations collided with opportunities.

A watershed moment for me was being asked to offer baseball sessions to interested kids in the Canadian Arctic in the summer of 2002. My dad had died that past February.

The Nunavut trips certainly helped expand my teaching of the game in diverse situations and stoked my love of travel again—this time by flight. While still in my twenties, I was selected as an Envoy Coach to represent Major League Baseball overseas—helping build the sport of baseball across the globe. I can now clearly see that injuring my shoulder—being propelled into coaching earlier than I had planned—was one of the best things that had ever happened to me in terms of baseball. Through MLB International's initiatives, nearly 30% of all players in Major League Baseball now come from countries outside the United States; the International Baseball Federation (IBAF) currently has over 115 baseball federations, up from 53 in 1993 and is played by over 35,000,000 people worldwide.

Envoys' roles were multi-faceted. In some cases Envoy trips were PR, and other times they included scouting, providing development camps, or troubleshooting and offering advice as federations needed. It was anything and everything. What I enjoyed most was establishing relationships with people from all over the world . . . all threaded together by baseball. They wanted to share their lives with me and their culture. Sold. When I had days off I milked them and, often serendipitously, found that most moments encountered are an education if you are willing to be the student.

The assignment choices that were offered to me for my first tour as a MLB Envoy were Germany, the Czech Republic, or a three country tour of Africa including Nigeria, Uganda and Zimbabwe. So it began. I had no idea I would be gone every summer for seven years up until my wife Melissa and I began our family. We joke now (or at least I do) that my

Team Great Britain versus Team Germany at a Cadet European Championship held in Lithuania.

'batting average' for being at home during our July 7th wedding anniversary our first years of marriage was .143 (1/7) due to baseball. I am glad she isn't into statistics.

Entering a Master's program in the States and becoming an assistant coach at a University during my studies seemed very appealing. My wife and I talked. Ultimately starting a family in the area was the magnet. We were ready. I had also been hit by 'writing lightning' in the Czech Republic on my last trip as an Envoy. I needed to combine my passions of travel, coaching baseball, and writing into one, and at the time, had also wanted to make more use of my English degree. I chatted with my wife through Skype while in the Czech Republic and ended up enrolling in a Writing Diploma offered at a university in my hometown: St. Peter's College. I wrote. And wrote. I received excellent guidance from my instructors. One of the stories I penned in an SPC class was submitted to the Saskatchewan Writers' Guild, which lead to a spot in their Mentorship Program—where I was matched with a Jedi of a professional editor, Ted Dyck. The majority of the essays and anecdotes in this collection were either written or polished during my productive times at St. Peter's and with my work with Ted.

The birth of our daughters Sarah and Leia caused me to reflect even more on what had happened over those eventful years with baseball. It also was a catalyst to mine other stories I had written connected to the game. Walter Friedman, of Summer Game Books, became involved and provided his valuable insight and expertise taking a chance on publishing the reshaped body of work as a collection.

The pieces contained in this book are not about me. Perhaps they aren't even really about baseball in a way. I think what they do reveal is that something valuable can be learned in pretty much every situation . . . and baseball itself can open doors to an intriguing classroom filled with remarkable people. For me, a little round ball has stitched acquaintances together from all over the world, and provided an opportunity to travel across three continents and form lifelong friendships in five. Even though languages spoken were sometimes foreign, fields were often makeshift, and skill levels varied from rookie to pro, there has always been comfort knowing that between the foul lines the fourth base on the diamond has been and always will be home. My favorite baseball writer, Bill Kinsella, said, "Baseball knows no limits, and on the true baseball field, the foul lines diverge forever, eventually taking in most, or all of the universe."

Qablunaaq on Hudson Bay

"A ship in harbor is safe . . . but that is not what ships are for."

—John A. Shedd

I was given the opportunity to offer introductory baseball clinics in Canada's Arctic after the community contacted Baseball Canada to 'try something new' for their summer youth programming. I flew up there for a couple of weeks over two summers. It remains as some of my most gratifying work and the day on Hudson Bay remains one of the truly unique trips I have ever taken.

Sebastian and Atuat take the guns out of the pickup and lean them against the side of the vehicle. The caliber of some are recognizable—but what type is the biggest one?

"What kind of gun is that?"

It sounds like Wayne says, "An Encase gun." What kind of brand is that?

"What's an Encase gun?"

"Just in case we *need* it. You never know what we might come across," Pujjuut says.

We push off the dock of the small Inuit community of Rankin Inlet—a hub of the Kivalliq Region—and float out on the water. The town of just over 2000 citizens was founded by a now defunct nickel mining operation in the 1950s, although the Thule Inuit inhabited the area for centuries prior. It is large considering there are only about 30,000 inhabitants in the entire territory. Nunavut, in Inuktitut, means 'our land' but this visitor thinks it means *cold*. Before venturing up to this area of the Arctic someone joked it had four seasons: June, July, August, and Winter.

Pujjuut Kusugak, my liaison during this trip, brought me over to his relatives—the Tootoo family—for a home cooked meal. I sampled many traditional dishes including fried caribou and onions which were *very* tasty. My appreciation to the cook was not shared, however. Before leaving Saskatchewan on this trip, I visited the local library and picked up a book on Inuit culture. A section outlined this advice: *Do not comment on the flavor of food or your pleasure gained from eating it. Food is not to be complimented or criticized—a living creature lost its life for your sustenance.* Some travel books aren't accurate. Whether this was factual or not . . . I did not chance being rude. I later forced a passport-photo-expression on my face after nibbling an undercooked and grayed caribou heart as a guest in another home. And hard-boiled Ptarmigan eggs: *never again.*

A northern version of baseball here is called *anauligaaq*—base runners are struck with a thrown ball instead of being tagged out which, not surprisingly, hurts just like it sounds. Imagine the stinging pain of being hit with a chucked ball in the Arctic cold. Or is your skin so numb at the time that the sensation of pain doesn't jolt you until later when you warm up indoors?

An introduction to the real game of baseball began after the Kivalliq Inuit Association wanted to try something *new* with its summer youth program. A mother involved, Bernadette Dean, at the urging of her son, Cody, felt that the game of baseball "like the Blue Jays on TV," would be interesting to introduce to local youth. Pujjuut, a summer student for the KIA, got on the internet, found Baseball Canada, and

The crushed rock infield at Rankin Inlet, Nunavut.

eventually decided that baseball would indeed be a good fit—arranging for sessions at Rankin Inlet, Baker Lake and Arviat. Greg Brons, Technical Director of Saskatchewan Baseball, called me up after having a call forwarded to him from Baseball Canada. I had been involved as a clinician and coach with the Prairie province's high performance programs—little did I know that baseball would lead me to Canada's Arctic.

The ball field itself sat plopped a foul ball away from Hudson Bay. It never got old seeing balls head that way. In all of my travels in the game I had never come across a field where ground balls were literally grounded when there were hit: they stopped dead shortly after colliding with the crushed rock infield. Literally . . . crushed rock. Needless to say, sliding drills were not on the activities list. I remembered learning about permafrost in elementary school but never did I dream that I would see a base tapped into it to secure it into the ground—it wasn't going anywhere.

Like many new to baseball, Wayne Kusugak struggled with hitting at first, and after practicing with him, I realized how interested he was in the game and his passion for it. Wayne listened and made adjustments. He hit his first homerun *ever* during last night's clinic . . . crushed it too. I couldn't help but think that they had missed the boat on the placement of the field as it would be a cool tradition to have to fish out rare homerun balls from Hudson Bay, rather than the water's edge serving as a foul line. The majority of the sessions were for youth, but I was more than happy to have adults for one in which they played a version of slow-pitch. It was interesting to see people that age so interested in learning more about improving their skill level.

It is early morning and now our two small boats are like *The Persephone* from the CBC television show *The Beachcombers*—aluminum, with a ramshackle wooden cabin area towards the middle. Heavy fog has prevented my flight from leaving, and no one really knows I am even still in town except for those at Tara's Bed and Breakfast, Pujjuut who navigates our craft, and his teenage cousin, Wayne, the homerun hitter. We are meeting up with Sebastian, Tommy Tanuyak, and Atuat Shouldice in the other boat. They are "after seal and beluga" and will accompany us on our trip to Marble Island. I am an invited guest and am honoured to travel to this intriguing destination. Perhaps they feel sorry for me that I am prevented from returning back to my family. Sebastian told me an interesting story when asked about his 'missing' Inuit last name: In 1969, the Government established 'Project Surname,' a two-year undertaking in which families *chose* their last name. Its purpose was to eliminate problems, frustrations, and difficulties with the existing government nomenclature for Inuit families—simplified with an E for east, W for west, ending in a string of numbers. Residents were visited and asked to pick unique surnames resulting in many families unable to reach a consensus on their new identity. Brothers within a family could essentially select a handful of different last names and still maintain their relational ties. Sebastian's family ended up with a tag that reflected his father's hairstyle: Curley.

Panning around in a complete circle—eyes widened and mouth open—nothing visible but water. Crisp fresh air. Deep inhalations. The sea—simply massive—melds with the sky, and like some dizzying blue blanket, wraps our small boat afloat the surprising sleepiness of Hudson Bay. Glassy water breaks when seals pop their heads up for air and bob, making small, circular ripples where they breathe. Singling out one seal after it surfaces, the boat with hunters quickly circles a broad area of about 100 meters; the seal goes underwater again. The boat loops, only tighter, closing the circumference. The pointed gun cracks with a gunshot at the lone, resurfaced seal. Harpooned quickly in case it will *kivik*—sink, Tommy pulls it towards the boat. What just occurred here? It takes two of the men to lift the slippery animal out of the water, resting half of the seal on the edge of the boat before a final burst of strength brings it entirely on board. Blood streams down, smearing the boat and pooling with the crimson circle of clouded water below. The seal, laid in a clear plastic box with no lid, is dead. Sebastian cuts a small incision in the seal's belly to prevent bloating; obviously, this is no trophy hunt for them. Judging by their plans for the seals, I know not one morsel will be wasted or taken for granted—continuing a tradition over 4000 years old. By the end of the morning, three seals are brought aboard their boat: a harp, ring and bearded seal (estimated at over five feet, 200 pounds). Sebastian, looking at the plastic box— now stained red—grins, "An Arctic zoo for this guy to see!"

The CB radio, with broken bits of Inuktitut and smatterings of English, announces other boats inquiring about how our day on Hudson Bay is shaping up. What is this Inuit word popping up, followed by giggles?

"What is kah-bloo-nah?"

"Qablunaaq," Pujjuut says.

"Whatever. What does it mean?"

"You."

"Me?"

"White guy. Qablunaaq means white man. You are a good luck charm today and other boaters joked that they want us to lend you to them for a while so they can have a good hunt too."

*   *   *

We are now off to Marble Island, a place of legend in the north, and a destination for the others to clean their catch.

As we near it, the appearance of the distant rock formation sheds light on its name: vanilla swirl shades of white rock poke out of the vast sea like huge chunks of marble.

Yesterday's fog. Imagine fog so thick that when you stretch your arm out you hit something that you didn't know was even in front of you. True story. Without the low fog the plane would have departed Rankin; a handful of passengers munching on stale pretzels, soaring overhead and looking down on what looked more like islands in water than anything else. The lingering haze led to a phone call from Pujjuut last night during rest at Tara's Bed and Breakfast, "Will you come with us to Marble? We are going out *on the land.*" I had overheard conversations about this mysterious island from locals standing near third base on the crushed rock infield at the field.

A voice cuts in, speaking the northern language to us over the CB radio. "We are in for a treat," Pujjuut says. He turns and sparks up another conversation, in Inuktitut, with Wayne.

"What did you just tell Wayne?"

"The reason we might not have seen any Beluga so far."

"Which is?"

"A *Bowhead!*" Pujjuut revs the boat's motor from its low hum to a roar.

Now, less than fifty meters from the shore of Marble Island, our boat slows to a trolling speed and drifts. The passengers in the companion boat nearby anxiously wait, as we do, for a sighting of the whale. Pujjuut details the Bowhead whale—an endangered species—and giant amongst giants. Its tadpole shape can grow over twenty meters (a length farther than pitcher to catcher) and it can live more than 100 years.

Bowheads tend to stay in shallow water as they move forward, ten-foot mouths agape, feeding on the smaller marine life passing through their baleen plates.

A dark hump slowly rises from the water. We grab the side of our boat and lean forward, eyeballs bulging, straining to get just one more inch nearer to this majestic creature. The whale's back rolls up, forward, and then wheels down below the surface. "Second time!" Wayne says, referring to the experiences he has had with a Bowhead in his life.

A picture snapped moments after a bowhead whale had surfaced.

Within meters of one of the rarest animals on earth—I ponder how easy it would be to hurl a baseball at it and *bean* it. I would never do such a thing, and as awe washes over me, I am embarrassed the thought even entered my mind. Always thinking something about baseball I guess.

"We need a permit—a license," Pujjuut replies when asked about the requirements for them to hunt a Bowhead. "Communities put in bids and when a Bowhead is successfully hunted, the meat is shared throughout all of Nunavut." A favorite way to eat this whale is to cut it into frozen slabs the size of a chocolate bar. Maktak, taken from the two-foot-thick whale blubber, is a good source of vitamin C and a traditional food of the territory, currently out of season in Rankin at this time of year.

Whale watching completed, we find a cove and drop anchor. Our boats, now tied together with rope, serve as makeshift cafeterias as we prepare an impromptu snack of tea, oysters, crackers, and nibs. A small Inuksuk on nearby Marble Island catches our attention. This rock formation is a

Smaller versions of this rock 'looks like a person' formation dot the landscape of the north.

dwarf in comparison to the photo-op Inuksuk within Rankin Inlet that towers over people at least double their size. These man-made landmarks, looking like small humans, dot the tundra and have deep roots in northern culture. Inuksuks are a welcome sight—an impression that more people are present here than six. Sebastian gestures, pointing to his right stating, "You will crawl on that land soon." He must be joking. "You will see."

Our conversation switches to the more than 15,000 caribou that trampled through Rankin two weeks ago. Small waves splashing against our idle boat interrupt the eerie calm—a contrast from the constant noise heard within the community of Rankin: dogs and all-terrain vehicles. The four-wheelers, always referred to as "Hondas," hum around the community non-stop. At this time of the year, people relish the daylight before the darkness looms over the long winter.

A tin of Copenhagen? Tobacco caps their midday snack as if it were an After Eight mint. My stomach rolls a bit. The price tag on the container reflects one of the realities of life in the North, the doubled cost of living. No chew for me. No way. A previous baseball experience *cured* any penchant I had for tobacco.

The warm tea, sun, and calm during our stop intensify the warmth of the insulated orange flotation suit I wear. Must unzip the top half. Instant relief. Earlier the question was offered why the qablunaaq was the only one wearing this get-up and why everyone else—sans coveralls—appeared underdressed. "We know what happens if we fall overboard . . . no chance. Wearing that suit helps keep sanity for first timers though." I dunk my hand into the sea. Frigid. Like digging for a canned drink at the bottom of a plastic cooler filled with ice.

16

The engine of our boat sputters a few times and then kicks in allowing us to continue towards the island. How clear the water becomes when it gets shallower. The number of creatures teeming, previously unseen below the surface, is astounding. We arrive on the shore and the seals are pulled onto the rocks. "Don't go too far," Sebastian warns. "You are going to crawl."

Looking back after crawling on hands and knees out of respect for a local custom.

A slow turn of the head, raising of an eyebrow, and a pause.

"You *are* serious?"

"Sure. You must crawl on your hands and knees to dry land. It is out of respect for the spirits that live here."

"You can do what you want," Pujjuut says, "but if you *don't* crawl, many believe you will be cursed with bad luck the rest of your life."

"Okay . . . why aren't you guys crawling then?"

"We have all been here before. You only have to do it on your *first* trip here."

Two accounts are given: When the whalers came from Europe they were so feeble, riddled with scurvy, famished and exhausted from their trans-Atlantic trip, that when they arrived at the island, they crawled from the shore to its dry land. The Inuit inhabitants of the island took the European travelers in and nursed them to good health. Visitors to Marble Island thereafter crawl ashore to relive that fateful moment of peril and show respect to the spiritual inhabitants who still lurk on the island. Another legend tells of an elderly woman who, not wanting to move with her family out of the area, pointed to the water proclaiming her wish to "live out on the ice that looked like an island." Years later, that family was said to have returned to the spot where they abandoned her only to hear a whispering voice say "the wish was granted" and that her "spirit now lives on this marble island." Being low to the ground, on hands and knees, is an act of respect for her. Not crawling is said to shorten your life.

I *need* to crawl.

The wet, jagged rock hurts my knees as though they are bare instead of wearing this orange suit. As I pull forward, each rough edge scrapes the palms of my hands. Where's the path with cushioning? Perhaps one covered in seaweed or any other type of green sludge would help. "You are cheating!" Sebastian yells observing my knees raised, body hunkering down like a bear to avoid contact with the stones. Laughter and comments in Inuktitut abound. This crawl will take longer than expected.

Finally, standing on the polished rock below, I soak in the surroundings making a complete rotation: the stillness of the water on Hudson Bay; the sepia and white rock of the island; sky fusing with the sea—fellow travelers downwind busying themselves with the catch. This moment will *never* be duplicated. A gust of wind. Crap! I almost fell.

*   *   *

Walking upright is better for the trek back. Slippery stones. Careful. Dodge the gaps in the rock to avoid re-spraining the ankle injured last week in Saskatchewan after being bowled over at home plate. Knives clang on sharpening tools. Blood is everywhere. The skins, sliced free from fat and meat, are removed intact, outlining the entire body of the seals—large enough for small blankets. Tommy, Pujjuut and Sebastian prove their cleaning of the seals is no rookie attempt. The meat is divided and bagged with nothing left to waste. How the food will be split up amongst the hunters is ignored as I am fixated on young Atuat who has taken the emptied intestines and is braiding them, remarkably with one hand, creating a creamy white weave that looks like a girl's twined hair. "It cooks better in soup and looks more presentable in the bowl this way," he claims. My stomach continues to rumble.

We stop before heading back to Rankin in an area where two vessels rest, permanently underwater, on the bed of a sheltered inlet. Pujjuut speaks of Captain James Knight and his crew of 40 men who lost their ships—*Albany* and *Discover*—here in the 1700's. These boats are assumed to have been broken up by ice during a wintery stop. Knight, a Hudson's Bay

Company explorer, was determined to find the Northwest Passage and spent what is thought to be two winters stranded on Marble Island. Deadman's Island is a nearby testament to the harsh reality of the northern seasons; graves are dug shallow, heaped above ground due to the frozen earth. Other remnants of past visitors include what is said to be the stone foundation of a theater that whalers used to entertain themselves. The legend of the sailors on the Knight Expedition stokes the mystique of Marble Island, located on the second largest bay in the world.

Don't forget the two baseballs. I pass them around to get scribbled messages in Inuktitut on. We are travelling back to the mainland. One ball, tucked in the pocket of my orange coveralls, and the other, hurled as far as possible into Hudson Bay. Will it ever be recovered?

The mind swims with images of this surreal day. Rough waves now. Hang on to something. The bow of our boat, held up in pop-wheel fashion, bounces across the water like a motorbike, full-throttle, on a pot-hole filled road. Flashes of memories of the seals, the bowhead whale, the crawling on Marble Island, the . . . are you kidding? The nose of our vessel drops. Shit! Water rushes up to the gunwales and we now drift the choppy sea with a dead engine.

Rocking with the waves, we trade glances, stunned. Sebastian, Tommy and Atuat motor *way* ahead of us. Our 6:30AM departure on the once peaceful water has evolved into a nightmarish moment in the increasing cold of 9PM on the icy water of Hudson Bay—breath visible like exhalations from a cigarette. A fear of the power of Mother Nature twists into undying *respect*.

*　　　*　　　*

What is colder—the hands or the face? It's *chilly*. Pujjuut pulls again on the cord of the motor like a frustrated kid trying to start a lawnmower. He takes the cover off of the engine and tinkers with various parts. Has this happened to him before? Perhaps we got away with something by avoiding motor issues earlier on our trip today. Not fond of the idea of having a frosty slumber party with these guys in the middle of nowhere. Especially in progressively colder temperatures. Fifteen minutes pass. What happened to the other boat?

How is Pujjuut even working on the pieces of the engine? His hands must be as numb as everyone's. A sputter and a puff of exhaust—the sound and smell of relief. We are on our way, heading towards Rankin Inlet, just as the fog begins to roll in again.

Have You Ever Heard of Jim Abbott?

"Kites rise highest against the wind, not with it."

—Winston S. Churchill

I travelled to the Czech Republic on my last summer tour with MLB before starting a family with my wife Melissa. While there we came across a young boy who dazzled us with his play despite a major challenge. His eyes lit up when I informed him of another player who overcame similar adversity and made it to the Big Leagues. I couldn't have made up what happened next.

Jim Fuller and I had spent the last three weeks traversing the Czech Republic as Envoy Coaches for Major League Baseball International. The majority of clubs we spent time with didn't mess around much when it came to equipment. I noticed this often in Europe: When people needed stuff they ordered the best right from the start . . . no messing around. The facilities were solid and one in particular, at Brno, stood out. It had a guest suite under the bleachers, a restaurant, bar, laundry

Team Japan and Team USA shake hands after playing a tournament held in the Czech Republic.

services, etc. where we stayed. I finally could say that I "lived at the park." The team there, Draci Brno, was one of the more successful teams in the land at the time and was sponsored by a local anti-virus company: AVG. Totally pro. It was there that Jim and I had V.I.P. credentials when the facility hosted *The World University Baseball Championships*. My highlight at that point: watching Stephen Strasburg sear the baseball over 100 MPH before being whisked away—the only amateur selected on Team USA—for the Beijing Olympics. He would be the first pick overall in the MLB draft the following year and of course go on to an impressive pro career. That memory was bumped to number two after I met David Farkas.

We met David on our second-to-last stop in a place called Blankso, a city of 20,000, two-and-a-half hours southeast of Prague—the day after we toured the Punkva Caves of the Moravian Karst, spelunking near the city on much needed time off. While chatting with baseball camp organizers and coaches in front of the third base dugout at Strawberry Field, my gaze was drawn towards the right field line where participants warmed up playing catch. One of the players had some kind of a skip in his step—or something—as he threw, playing long toss, with his partner. I kept glancing over to that area during a conversation I was having with camp staff. Eventually, curiosity pulled me to saunter down and see what was going on. I was surprised and very impressed that the boy with the skip was playing catch with only one hand. He threw with his right hand, and then snagged his glove from under the stub of his left arm that ended just below the elbow. Thrusting his throwing hand into the glove, he caught the ball, stuck his glove back under his left armpit, pulled the ball out with his right hand, and threw it back to his partner—all seamlessly and remarkably, with one arm.

I approached him and asked, "Have you ever heard of Jim Abbott?" His face was totally blank. My excitement had led me to temporarily forget that I was in a foreign country and that most people, especially children, did not understand English very well. I yelled for one of our helpers on the field: "Jans! Jans! Ask him if he ever heard of a Major League Baseball player named Jim Abbott?"

The young boy's head shook a simple, uninterested no. Abbott was a popular player who made his debut in 1989 with the California Angels—one of only a few who went straight to the Big Leagues from college. He pitched for several MLB teams, including the New York Yankees, with whom he threw a no-hitter. Growing up, I was a fan of Abbott's, and like many, was amazed how he had overcome so much adversity to make the Majors, having been born missing the bottom of an arm and with only one hand, just like David.

The information about Abbott was translated to David and the twelve year old's jaw dropped and his mouth spread wide into a toothy grin. Flies could have landed on his tongue. It was one of my most heartwarming memories from Europe. "I think I will like *this* guy!" Jans translated back to me from David. Giddy, heading back towards the gathered coaches, I bee-lined to Jim Fuller, a retired college coach and my partner—an Envoy Coach for over a decade. Jim, 64 and a former catcher, had had his share of knee injuries in his career. He threw batting practice like a programmed robot and often told people he was "old school." I admired his strong work ethic and endless (read: awesome) drills. After I told him of the young boy, Jim replied, "Super! I will have to get a hold of Jimmy and let him know about David."

Jim Abbott pitched for four different MLB teams from 1989 to 1999.

"You *know* Jim Abbott?"

"Sure. I coached him at the Baseball Center I ran for the city of Flint, Michigan. He was just a bit younger than David is right now. Jim Abbott was a stand-out high school athlete . . . he was an excellent baseball player and also a starting quarterback in high school football. Did you know that he was quite the hitter too?" I cocked my head to the side contemplating how hard it would be to even make contact with a well thrown pitch, hitting one-handed. "He was a late pick by the Toronto Blue Jays in 1985, went to play at the University of Michigan, and was later re-drafted by the Angels as a first-rounder in 1988. Jimmy was the winning pitcher when the United States won gold at the '88 Olympics—their first ever in baseball. Jim Abbott is one of the most modest and polite persons I have ever been around."

We would later see David play *shortstop* where he fielded ground balls and threw out runners with ease at the park named after the strawberry patch it was built on top of. He hit too. He couldn't generate much power yet, but the fact that he even put the ball in play—with one arm—was remarkable to me. To the other kids David was like everyone else and they treated him as such. Our sessions continued with us working ten hour days—from 9AM-3PM with the kids' camp and 6-10PM with the top adult team . . . all in scorching heat.

Eventually we left Blansko for a week at Hlouboka where we worked with an all-star team that was preparing for a major tournament. I had to leave that camp just prior to its end as I needed to return to Canada to begin teaching— the start of the school year only days away. Soon after, Jim Fuller sent me an email; included was a copy of the following letter:

Dear David,

A friend of mine and a great coach, Mr. Jim Fuller told me about some of your accomplishments on the baseball diamond. Your story brought back a lot of memories for me, *because I was just like you when I was your age. I was born missing my **right** hand (so we are a little different). But I grew up loving the game of baseball and determined to figure out different ways of playing, so that I could play on the same teams as the rest of my friends.*

It took a lot of practice and effort, but you know what? I ended up playing in the Major Leagues! I played for the California Angels, the New York Yankees and a few other teams. Sometimes I still can't believe that those dreams came true. So I just wanted to write you a note and wish you the best of luck. I know it isn't easy being different. I know it is very hard to have to do things differently than other kids. But if you can find your own way, make the most of your abilities, and always believe in yourself, dreams can come true! Always believe that.

Tough challenges make special people . . . David you will always be special and you will always be up to any challenge. Someday, I look forward to hearing about all of your amazing accomplishments.

Thanks for taking the time to read this. Please let me know if I can ever help you. By the way did I mention that my grandparents are Czech! So we have a lot of things in common.

Wishing You the Best,

Jim Abbott

Just a Ball

"No person was ever honored for what he received. Honor has been the reward for what he gave."

—Calvin Coolidge

I had first heard about Father Mathew's ball when I was in junior high. Twenty years later I decided to write a story about it for a non-fiction writing class that I was taking at St. Peter's—the very grounds where he spent the majority of his life. Impact. Father Mathew made an impact ... as did a little round ball on him.

That I forgot about the ball surprises me considering how *big* it is. It has fingerprints from admirers across North America and has been handled by some of the biggest stars to ever play the game as well. I first heard about it when I was in Grade 7 and was intrigued by it as a youngster, more so when its keeper died during my first semester of university in 1994. My father was a grain farmer and, with his brother Murray, operated Loehr's Trenching—excavating with a backhoe, digging basements, installing water lines and providing other infrastructure work. As a service, they also dug graves for families in the area. Dad told me he had recently buried Father Mathew Michel; it was then that he told me more of the story about that ball.

Twenty years after first hearing about the baseball in Grade 7, now a teacher of that grade, and an expectant father, the memory of the ball flashes before me. I am looking for material to write about for a University class I am enrolled in. I have come to realize that there are often stories within a story. I also need to to see for myself if what dad said about the baseball is true. It is not exactly an exhausting journey as the ball lies less than a mile away my entire life, though I have never seen it.

St. Peter's, on the outskirts of Muenster, Saskatchewan.

St. Peter's Abbey, a Benedictine monastery on the out-skirts of the greenery surrounding Wolverine Creek, is south of the railroad tracks from the village of Muenster, Saskatchewan. The Abbey is serenity incarnate and the final home for the ball. A brief conversation last week with Abbot Peter Novecosky has pointed me in the direction of Father Leo Hinz, curator of the archives.

I have been waiting in the reception area for a few minutes. Fr. Leo slowly walks in, "Hello, Mervin," he says. A warm feeling washes over me. Older people often inadvertently call me by my dad's name, even though he died years ago. He quickly corrects himself. "No problem," I offer, "I am used to it."

Descending to the basement by elevator, Father Leo reaches for the light of the musty room, extends his arm and points to the back wall. "There is where the ball is," he says, as he slowly moves his arm across himself to point to the mass storage shelves filled with files, "and here is where you can find out more about Michel's life."

I sheepishly walk toward the container on the shelf, like a youngster waiting to meet a big leaguer for the first time. Then I stop.

Father Leo notices my pause and asks, "You want to learn about Michel first don't you?"

I feel I should.

He makes a space for me, moving jumbled papers and letters to the edges of a nearby table. The cardboard box, labeled 'Arthur' with black magic marker, is in my hands; the tape holding his obituary card is losing sticking power, barely keeping the memorial note in place. I plunk the container, which safe guards remnants of Father Mathew's life, into the middle of the work area and pull a file at random from the unsorted box.

"What you called him sounded like Michael?"

"Yes" the aging priest says, "M-I-C-H-E-L is pronounced like the name Michael. A lot of people get it wrong."

I learn, after scanning the initial sheet drawn, that Michel received his secondary education in Collegeville, Minnesota. I am familiar with this area, within Stearns County, as it is near the original settlement of my ancestors. My forefathers, after living in the United States for over 60 years, ventured north to what would later become Saskatchewan, with the Benedictine monks; their eventual destination, later officially called Muenster, was not yet incorporated as a village. My ancestors loved baseball, as evidenced by one of the first team pictures of a ball team taken in the area. The black-and-white portrait freezes in time four men with bowler hats and ten players in full uniform, four of whom I am related to. The love of the game was passed on from John Loehr Sr. to his son Arnold, who in turn passed it to my grandfather Irwin, then my father Mervin, myself, and I am sure my future children. Considering that, obviously, Father Mathew never married, I hope his legacy can be shared and the story of his baseball passed on through the generations as well.

Flipping through further pages I learn that about the same time that photo was taken, a young Arthur Michel was completing high school, and growing a love for the game of baseball. A few years later, in 1916, Arthur would further his studies in Collegeville, at St. John's University, and be drafted to a different Big League, joining the Benedictine community in St. Peter's Monastery, in Muenster. He would choose the name Mathew upon his ordination in 1921.

"Father—what do *you* remember about Father Mathew?"

The resonant hum of the lights is drowned as Father Leo says, cocking his head to the side, "He was a *determined* man. What he said he would do . . . he did. He was big and strong. Michel was known for riding miles and miles to church on horseback—even in the dead of winter." The little I had heard from other people about Father Mathew was mixed including his imposing personality, stubbornness, and strong will.

"How did he come across the ball?"

"School in the States."

Father Leo, now resting on a rickety stool, points to the end wall where the ball rests. As I walk reverently toward the shelf I feel like I am at a wake—nervous to glimpse into the coffin. I reach for a simple charcoal-gray, cardboard box, which is too small to hold a single shoe. Scotch Tape holds each corner together and secures a manila card on the lid, labeling its contents. It seems (to me) like an irreverent final resting place for a piece of history pregnant in baseball lore. A printed name on the bottom of the card, boldly scribbled over itself a few times, spells out: *Fr. MATHEW.* Gingerly lifting the lid, I peer in. An ordinary baseball, yellowed over the years, appears. I leave it lie.

I am shocked as I read a small card inside listing the signatures of various players who signed the ball: most impressive, *Babe Ruth.* Fourteen other Yankees etched their names; George Pipgras, Benny Bengough, Roy Sherid, Tony Lazzeri, Johnny Grabowski, Leo Durocher, Bill Dickey, Lou Gehrig, Lyn Lary, Herb Pennock, Bob Swawkey, Art Jorgens, "Dusty" Rhodes, and Cedric Durst.

This picture deserves closer scrutiny after you have read the entire story.

Unbelievable. I knew Babe Ruth signed it—but Gehrig too!

"Nothing can leave the archives. If you want, I can make a few copies of files for you if something stands out in particular."

The ball remains in the box as I begin rummaging through the container of files, scribbling relevant dates: 1896, 1921, 1929, 1948, 1987, 1994.

"I am *sure* there was a newspaper article written about Father Mathew and the ball," I say, leafing through the filed pages. "I remember reading it. I was in Grade 7 and that was when I learned about the ball for the first time."

"You are always welcome to come back. I do have to get going early today. Sorry."

"No problem. I *need* to come again though. I have to take some pictures and also check something out more closely."

*　　　*　　　*

At home, the desk in my basement office is covered with sticky notes and tidily stacked research as I reassemble the puzzle of his life for myself. The material gathered on Father Mathew now includes a newspaper story, parish history books, articles written by the Abbey, parish newsletters, and his obituary. I have become fascinated by his life. I am surprised to read that he was chosen as the *first* principal of St. Peter's College in 1921 and received his inaugural parish assignment that same year—all at age 25. A spellbinding picture in a 1981 article written by Abbot Peter titled *Father Mathew: 60 years a priest,* shows the Reverend bundled in black and riding on horseback—just as Father Leo mentioned.

Another date I wrote down during my first visit with Father Leo rises up from the pile in the form of a note left by Father Mathew: *In 1928 I was sent to do graduate studies at the Catholic University of America (CUA), Washington, D.C. After a few months I was made head supervisor of a student's residence on the CUA campus. My card designated me as President of Albert Hall. This card, together with my keen interest in baseball, won me a pass to all American League games, a seat near the players' dugouts, and eventually the cordial acquaintance of Babe Ruth* (June 1, 1987).

The letter indicates the Philadelphia Athletics were the Yankee's opponent that day. The fall contest, in 1929, took place just before the Stock Market Crash (and impending dust bowl of the Great Depression). I do a quick Google search and discover that the Yankees were the defending back-to-back World Series Champions and Connie Mack's

Athletics would later win the title that season. The A's boasted Jimmie Foxx, Mickey Cochrane, Al Simmons, Max Bishop and Lefty Grove. The Yankees, who were one of two teams that year to introduce the practice of permanently using numbers on their jerseys, had a roster brimming with talent, including Leo Durocher, Bill Dickey, Lou Gehrig and of course The Babe.

John Goodman. I remember a film called *The Babe*— starring John Goodman—where the slugger is influenced by priests in his formative years. Not having a copy of this movie sparks my memory of something better. Climbing the stairs up from our basement, I head towards to my collection of books. Years ago, I bought a first edition paperback (1948) called *The Babe Ruth Story* at a thrift store for 25 cents. I have not read it until now. Through it I deduce that—as a boy—George Herman Ruth was ignored. He was reared in his father's saloon near where Oriole Park at Camden Yards (Baltimore's current field) now stands. Ruth often spent time roaming neighborhood streets. From this raw upbringing he was sent at the age of seven to an industrial school for boys. "It was at St. Mary's," Ruth writes, "that I met and learned to love the greatest man I've ever known."

At St. Mary's Industrial School for Boys, operated by the Xaverians, a Catholic order that worked with the underprivileged, Ruth found his surrogate family. Brother Matthias, a quiet man who took on a paternal role, introduced Ruth to the game of baseball and built up the youngster's arsenal of tools. Despite his intimidating size (estimated in the book to be 6'6", 250 lbs.) Brother Matthias became a hero to Ruth, teaching him to read and write and the difference between right and wrong. Brother Matthias, as busy as he was at St. Mary's, made Ruth feel like he mattered and Ruth responded to his firm, guiding hand.

The Babe recalled, "I never would have played it professionally if Brother Matthias hadn't put me in my place one day and changed not only my position on the field but the course of my life." Ruth was laughing at his team's pitchers who struggled on the mound and were continually replaced. Brother Matthias, within earshot of the taunting, called "Time!" and promptly forced the delinquent Ruth to pitch, to prove a point. "He did it to

There appears to be a certain twinkle in Fr. Mathew's eye when holding the ball for all to see.

take me down a notch," said Ruth. "Brother Matthias saw to it that I didn't get far away from the pitcher's box during my last two seasons at St. Mary's."

By 1914, Ruth—at age 19—had passed through the exit and entrance of St. Mary's repeatedly. His talents had grown exponentially and his name became known to Jack Dunn, a baseball owner, who signed him. George Herman Ruth would never forget the lessons learned at St. Mary's and the impact of his mentor.

*   *   *

A couple of hours at Humboldt's Reid Thompson Library, cranking through rolls of microfilm from the late 1940's, pays off. Father Mathew Michel was instrumental in implementing electrical service on farms in the area—so much so he was dubbed "Father of Rural Electrification." His strong will polarized some, but it was the end result that mattered most. On another microfilm I see something that gives me pause. At the bottom of an article I so desperately sought—*Electric Power Comes to Annaheim*—is another story on the same page titled *Loehr Recommends Improvements of Highway 20*. My great-grandfather Arnold Loehr is interviewed for an article just after he was elected as a Member of the Legislative Assembly. After all this time searching through these films, what are the chances of coming across a nugget like that?

*   *   *

The internet, a couple of baseball encyclopedias, a Humboldt Journal, and a Saskatoon Star-Phoenix newspaper article (from the time I was a student in Grade 7) help me to understand the events of 1929. A mythic figure world wide, The Babe transcended baseball circles and was *the* American pop-culture icon. Ruth, who batted third in the order, wore the corresponding number 3, stitched in navy blue on the back of his grey Yankee jersey. He was paid a league-high $70,000 in 1929, hit .345, knocked in 154 RBI's, and was on his way to winning his tenth homerun title with forty-six round-trippers.

Despite the bustling routines of the professional baseball game that afternoon, The Sultan of Swat sauntered over to a man he observed talking to an usher near the Yankee dug-out. It was Father Mathew, courtesy pass in hand and wear-ing a long black cassock complete with white clerical collar. I wonder if a flash of Brother Matthias struck Ruth when he viewed Father Mathew in the distance?

The Bambino asked Fr. Mathew if he had a baseball with him. Ruth plucked one that was being used in batting practice and signed it: 'Babe Ruth'. Talking ball with Father Mathew, Ruth was peppered with the Reverend's baseball knowledge, love of the Yankees, and recollection of game statistics. Then he called his teammates over and they scrawled their signa-tures on the ball—a gift from The Babe to the Father.

Father and Babe ended their impromptu gathering, parting company due to the impending game. Many of the players on the field that day landed in the Baseball Hall of Fame—mak-ing the meeting even more memorable—but it was Ruth, who with the small act of taking time out for someone, left the priest with a stadium of memories and a baseball memento Father Mathew would revere the rest of his life.

*   *   *

I pick up the Babe Ruth autobiography a few days later and read about one accomplishment that escaped his grasp: to become manager of the New York Yankees. His career wrapped up after he was signed as a free agent by the Boston Braves in 1935. It was his final season. His life's work was sealed with his induction in the newly created Baseball Hall of Fame the following year. In the mid-to-late 1940's, while Father Mathew was working on 'bringing power to the peo-ple,' Ruth fought for his life; the once mighty slugger's health was in steady decline after being diagnosed with cancer in November of 1946.

The following spring, on April 27th, 1947 the Yankees held 'Babe Ruth Day.' The baseball legend, using a bat as a cane, spoke with a raw voice of his heartfelt passion for the game. His famed number 3 was retired—11 days before my great-grandfather was elected as MLA—June 13th, 1948—Ruth's last appearance in public before his death two months later.

*   *   *

Father Mathew Michel—whose vocation had a legacy in its own right—earned a Doctorate in Education at the Catholic University of America and enlightened over a dozen parishes during his long-standing service within the Abbacy of St. Peter's in Saskatchewan. Throughout his life, he never forgot his brush with Babe or the gift he received from him. The autographed ball, often kept at his desk and made accessible to any inquiring mind, was a conversation piece shared with most visitors. Perhaps if George Herman Ruth would have known the impact Father Mathew would make in people's lives, The Babe might have asked for *his* signature that fateful day.

Father Mathew's ball, a token of his moment with Babe Ruth, was handled by countless admirers, dirtied hands and all, and was shared spanning eras of Pius VI to John Paul II, Mackenzie King to Chretien, Hoover to Clinton, Kenesaw Mountain Landis to Bud Selig. Father Mathew accomplished many of the goals he set to achieve—all, that is, but one: his aspiration to blow out the candles on his 100th birthday cake. He fell three years short when he died on January 22, 1994. This was my first semester of college baseball. During a phone call home, my father informed me of Father Mathew's passing—and told me what he had heard about the ball.

*   *   *

I need another trip to the basement archives—this time with a digital camera and a print out from the internet.

"Here is a picture of a Babe Ruth autograph on a ball."

"You don't believe Fr. Mathew's ball is real?" Father Leo asks as though I have said something blasphemous.

"I believe it. I guess I printed it because it was so accessible on the computer."

I pull out my camera and take a picture of the small, gray box. I slowly lift out the ball and hold it at arm's length, snapping pictures of each part of the ball's horseshoe threads. My father, years ago in 1994, had told me that he heard that some-one, for whatever reason, had traced over the signatures that were fading. I scrutinize the ball as I roll it around slowly, scanning it in my fingers. It's true. I shake my head as it is apparent that a number of autographs have been touched up—by various pens—as if to grasp memories that were sim-ply slipping away. I breathe a sigh of relief as 'Babe Ruth', an exact replica of the internet print-off, is clearly intact in its original stroke.

I reflect on the fingerprints that have contributed to the fading of this baseball. If it was *my* ball, it would have been in a glass display case from day one. But this was not Father Mathew's way. He was not afraid of the ball getting touched—he insisted on it. This sharing of the baseball allowed *it* to do the touching. The ball carries with it an emotional impact that Father Mathew cherished and others will revere. Father Mathew wanted the gift to keep on giving and, no matter what, the ball always will be wrapped tight in legendary memories as great as the icons involved.

Blame Joe

"Only two things are infinite, the universe and human stupidity, and I'm not sure about the former."

—Albert Einstein

The second of the Toronto Blue Jays championship wins featured one of the most exciting endings in the history of the World Series. Looking back, I now realize that I totally ditched my father at home on the couch, after having watched each and every moment of the series up to that point with him . . . all for the lure of the action and what might occur if the Jays won. Turns out the after-party evolved into one of the more embarrassing things I have ever witnessed relating to baseball. The Blue Jays did not win another World Series while my dad was still alive, and in fact have not been to the postseason since.

Even those who hadn't watched much baseball that season—or ever for that matter—were spellbound each and every game of the 1993 World Series: Toronto versus Philadelphia. "How about those Blue Jays!" was prevalent in many Canadian conversations that year and, for a change, the nation had buzzed over something other than who had snapped the

#29 makes history in October of 1993.

puck into the waiting twine of a net. Fans hoped that the Toronto Blue Jays would return as champions of Major League Baseball.

The game that clinched the title had represented another opportunity—P-A-R-T-Y—and no one had wanted to miss out. Apparently last year when the Jays won a few spontaneous parties erupted on Eighth Street in Saskatoon, the province's largest city, located just over an hour from my hometown. We had thought that if the Jays repeated as champions on that October night, it was anyone's guess what would happen, and I unquestionably witnessed it . . . even though I now regret it.

A hometown girl who attended the University of Saskatchewan had offered her residence for the festivities that night in Saskatoon, since her rented home was conveniently located just off of Eighth Street. They had a lot to clean up the next morning; a gathering of her friends had evolved into a throng of other peoples' friends and, of course, their friends. I couldn't help but feel that the noise of the party in the room was disrespectful to a game of that magnitude. Don't talk during the sermon.

I had watched Gretzky pass it to Lemieux in 1987, Dave Ridgeway kick it through the uprights during the 89' Grey

Cup, numerous political election battles, Toronto's inaugural World Series championship win in 1992 and other events—all with Dad. My days at the home—where I had grown up my entire life—were numbered. I had tendered offers to play college baseball in the midwestern United States and narrowed my choice down to a few universities. I now know that night was one of the last opportunities (other than the Federal Election that took place the following Monday) to share a major TV event with Dad before he died. I truly miss the tidbits, bantering, and witty remarks he offered whenever we watched virtually any show type of show together. Come to think of it, he gave those types of comments about everything, all the time . . . and I loved it.

The 1992 series was the first MLB championship played outside of the United States and the first that a non-American club had won—a bona fide "World Series." Dad swore out loud every time when the Atlanta Braves faithful, 50,000 strong, chanted their Tomahawk Chop like programmed robots. His head had turned beet-red when, during game two of that series, the United States Marine Corps Color Guard accidently hoisted the Canadian flag upside down during the pre-game anthems.

Dad. The guilt. I had *bailed* on him.

The serenity of our rural Saskatchewan home in Muenster wouldn't have been as lively as that shindig in the city that night. I had become imprisoned within the walls of that small living room in Saskatoon and had attempted to keep my eyes focused on the elderly 24 inch television as I watched the Philadelphia Phillies and Blue Jays. Kind of comical looking back on it now, as I don't think I would watch a game that important unless it was in HD and with a screen over 60 inches.

Most people at the party had been there strictly for a bash and not to watch one of the most exciting World Series in a generation. I had come for both, although I was mainly there for the latter. *"All I can say is that my life is pretty plain, Ya don't like my point of view . . . that I'm insane."* Blind Melon. There was no escaping that song "No Rain." Every time I hear it now I think of that night. I know damn sure it didn't play at my parents' house during the ball game—Dad's only interruption at home had likely been to get up and go to the can.

*   *   *

I did not hear the broadcast very well above the cheers—anticipation was growing for a Blue Jay win.

"Who hit the triple?" a voice called from the kitchen.

"Molitor!"

It was difficult to concentrate in that raucous atmosphere. Conversations about trivial things, the bass that vibrated through the walls of the next room, and a few people simply too LOUD were a distraction to the few, like me, who had wanted to focus on the game itself. A roar resonated when Joe Carter hit a sacrifice fly and scored Paul Molitor. I had sat captive, cross-legged on the worn carpet that had had more than its fair share of drinks spilled on it over the years. I remember imagining Dad: prone on the chesterfield, gingerly tapping his cigarette into his glass ashtray, routinely pausing at unscheduled intervals for sips of cold Molson Canadian and cussing periodically at the TV screen whenever Philadelphia got a hit. I certainly could have actually *watched* the game if I had been there with him.

Many at that house in the city were oblivious, due to partying, that Dave Stewart (with his cold, intimidating death stare) chucked a gem. He only gave up a run on two hits through six innings. The Jays had bashed a homer in the fifth and added to their lead. A bottle cap had zoomed past my unprotected eyes—snapped for distance by the thumb and middle finger of an ignorant partier across the room. Someone performed a taste-test on one of the house plants.

A win in Game 6 meant back-to-back World Series titles for the Toronto team. Blue Jay fan's had ached for that feat—not accomplished by any team in Major League Baseball since the New York Yankees, fifteen years earlier, in 1978. It was a chance to show that the 1992 win was not some random fluke.

Chairs, laps, and every square inch of floor had been claimed for the end of the game. The aroma of body odor and hairspray swirled together and permeated the room.

I shook my head when the TV announcer commented on the craze that the Blue Jays had caused across Canada. Toronto was the only baseball team we had read about, heard about, or seen on sports casts in the west. The Montreal Expos had had their ups and downs, but did not receive the true national coverage they deserved. The Jays had become *Canada's Team.* That year alone Toronto had over 4 million fans spin the turnstiles—Major League Baseball's fifth highest attendance figure of all time.

"It's close now," I said to a friend, who had arrived late to that party. "We're down 6-5. Molitor hit one out in the fifth.

We were actually up 5-1 for a while. The wheels fell off in the seventh when we went through three pitchers—Dykstra crushed a three run homer. Five runs in that inning!"

"You're kidding."

"Nope."

The Phillies lanky closer Mitch Williams—6'4", hillbilly mullet—had thrown gas. The Philadelphia pitcher's unorthodox style was so erratic, I had wondered if batters simply stood there, that the *Wild Thing* might have walked the runners in to lose that game.

After a squandered eighth without a spark of offense, the unlikelihood that the Jays would pull it off, sobered me. Down one with one out in the bottom of the ninth, after having blown a five run lead, a seventh and deciding game had seemed likely to many that night.

Joe. If anyone could do it, it was him. Joe Carter's sweet stance exuded potential power each time he stepped to the plate. He batted from the right side and with the Blue Jays down 6-5 in the bottom of the ninth, the count 2-2, and number 29 in his familiar batting posture, I had closed my eyes and offered a silent prayer, opening them on cue for Carter's crucial cut at the ball.

"Now the 2-2. Well hit . . . down the left field line . . . way back . . . and gone! Joe Carter with a three-run homer! The winners and still *World Champions*—the Toronto Blue Jays!"

Broadcaster Sean McDonough's call on that swing brought drawn out, thunderous cheers. Hypnotized by the moment, everyone had to digest what had been witnessed with hungry eyes. *It* had happened. H-O-M-E-R-U-N!

Stunned to silence, I had been fixated on Joe as he trotted around the bases. I had yearned for the base paths to stretch from Victoria to St. John's. 360 feet seemed too short a distance to run for a walk-off, come-from-behind, game-ending blast in the bottom of the ninth, in his home park, *to win the World Series*. A scenario like that had *never* played out in the long annals of Major League Baseball history—it was legend time. If the Blue Jays had been a political party, a coronation would have occurred in the following Monday's election—a landslide win, with Joe Carter Canada's new Prime Minister—via Jays fans' votes.

*   *   *

The front entrance door slams as a few more people from the party head onto Eighth Street into the crisp, fall night. As a Coke commercial ends—a jingle in tribute to the Jays victory—we grab our coats and follow others. The cool air refreshes as it hits my cheeks, and I realize how stale and stuffy the last few hours had been. We are a chorus of screaming fools and a magical Saskatoon sky twinkles above us.

On Eighth Street, euphoria vibrates in the air as we make our way down the sidewalk catching the initial glimpses of jubilation occurring mere minutes after the win. Cars and trucks honk and bleat like high-flying geese. Vehicles pass by, passengers with arms dangling out of windows, single fingers raised in number one with record numbers of high-fives as trucks pull to the side to contact pedestrians. How can so many strangers bond like this?

People continue to spill onto Eighth Street. Canadian flags dominate the air, raised proudly in clenched fists. Two people scurry ahead of me with the red and white draped over their shoulders like capes—transforming 'Everyday Joes' into superhero form. It's nuts. A few minutes earlier, Carter had been mobbed at home plate by his teammates and now, vicariously, united as one, fans encircle each other like long-lost friends. Hugs, high-fives and cheers with total strangers are exchanged as though we are on the field, embracing members of our Blue Jay team.

*　　*　　*

It's funny, I have been out here for over an hour and have only bumped into people from the house party a few times. You can't really stay together in this mass of people—jumping onto the boxes of half-tons with total strangers tends to separate you a bit. I am not sure I like this. Cops? What are they doing mixing in with the crowd? I bet *they* missed the game. I slip my way in-and-out through crowds until I am finally close to a police officer. The sting of his bear paw-like slap meets mine with little delay when I raise my hand, palm open, in a celebratory high-five.

"Did you see it? Did you see Joe mash it?"

"I wish—listened to Tom Cheek's play-by-play on the radio though."

The device clipped to his uniform bleeps repeatedly as voices interrupt in mysterious codes. The officer responds back in a numerical language that is equally foreign to me. Something is going on.

"We expected a ton of people here because of last year's party, but this is ridiculous. Someone radioed before that they think over 6,000 people are here."

Who can anticipate the number of fans that will pour onto the street after their team wins the championship? Youth full of liquid courage—senses numbed and with a mob mentality—are starting to emerge. A glass bus stop is overturned, shattering its walls. Why? Cops on foot, on bikes, and in front of patrol cars—lights flashing—are ever-present. Why would anyone even try that crap when the police are right here? Are they rebelling against their presence? Are they simply too intoxicated?

A buzzing swarm grows as lines form outside late-night businesses. Management begins to click the locks on their doors. I guess now is not the time to think of potential profits but rather of protecting wares from sticky-fingered loiterers. Trucks jammed with passengers continue to creep down the street. Chants of 'Back-to-back!' 'OK . . . OK . . . Blue Jays . . . Blue Jays!' echo in the distance. "Whoomp, there it is!" Whoomp, there it is!"

My throat is raw. The palms of my hands are hot and sore from slapping what seems like 10,000 hands tonight. I think I popped in and out of 25 different cars and trucks celebrating with people—strangers for eternity. An hour and a half passes by in what seems like minutes. Punk. What is that idiot trying to prove? Down the sidewalk someone is repeatedly jumping on the top of a car at a dealership on Eighth. No need to intervene: someone squeezes his large frame from a hiding spot—under a nearby vehicle—and throws an impressive flurry of haymakers onto the pitiful kid.

Looking down the street, silhouettes are dangling, blocking the view of the amber, green, and red traffic lights as people hang from the towering green pole. I can't help but shake my head. Pressure must be being applied from somewhere as the forward momentum of the crowd has bottlenecked. Fans are not retreating.

Word spreads like a prairie brush fire that the police have made *the* decision. Riot Act. How did it come to this? It appears a single police officer, his voice crackling through a miniscule loudspeaker, tries to imply to thousands, "Go home." Cops mix in the crowd, stern expressions on their faces, as they attempt to officiate. This is getting stupid: Time to go.

Clouds of what appears to be smoke begin to billow in the distance. How could there be a fire in the middle of the street? A knowing glance is all it takes—there will never be a chance for a friend and I to witness this again in our squeaky-clean, law-abiding lives. A few others from the house party and I make our way toward the smudge. Up close the fumes are an odd fusion of greenish and yellow tinge blended with shades of white—like when people throw things they shouldn't into fire pits. There is no way I am leaving without getting a snootful. Just a small, sharp whiff of the substance, enough to surrender to the sting, makes my eyes water instantly. Tear gas. The *pain*. I clutch my nose grasping for what feels like a wooden match that was struck, blown out, and then immediately jammed deep into my nostrils to smolder. I have had enough entertainment on this night and now it needs to become a memory.

Through the haze I can see the moving wall of officers. They are dressed identically, like a team: black polished boots, matching helmets with visors snapped down. In one hand they hold long black billy clubs, ready to swing like bats, the other, clear half-body shields with POLICE decaled across them. The force slowly marches side-by-side in unison, blocking pitched beer bottles as they push forward towards the swarm.

I am astonished at how young partiers managed to function in the thousands a short time ago, and now a number of them will end their night screaming at, kicking, and throwing bottles at police officers—all the while being beaten away with sticks. I wonder how they would have replied if, during the ballgame, a friend leaned over and whispered prophetically in their ear, "You will sleep in the crowbar hotel later tonight."

Dad is not going to believe this. He will be disappointed to know I was even here. Turning around in disgust I head towards the house. How did this happen? A single swing of a bat resulted in a full scale riot, arrests, injury, and thousands of dollars of damage. Blame Joe.

Over a million people congregated in Toronto after the Blue Jays won in 1993, yet only a handful of incidents occurred there under that congestion. Saskatoon, Saskatchewan embarrassingly dotted media reports, across Canada and parts of the United States, with news of the bedlam on Eighth Street. October 23rd, 1993 was an infamous night, so much so that Saskatoon's first, and short-lived, pro baseball team in 1994 received the dubious moniker of the 'Riot'.

The following Monday Conservative Kim Campbell went down in one of the greatest defeats in Canadian election history to the Liberal's Jean Chrétien. I had redeemed myself watching that all go down with family at home. I think it was a more meaningful 'win' for my dad that night anyway. It was certainly more peaceful than a couple of days prior. I couldn't help but think that Joe Carter likely received a good number of write in votes, too.

Hitters are Like Snowflakes

"Success is peace of mind which is a direct result of self-satisfaction in knowing you did your best to become the best you are capable of becoming."

—John Wooden

I walked through Paderborn, Germany with The Torch one night after getting lost with him during an Envoy trip. I wish I could have spent more time with Tony Torchia as he was a wizard of sorts, with his endless knowledge of the game and wisdom drawn from life experiences. He certainly changed my perspective on what success means.

Internet access when I travel overseas with baseball is the most important link to life back home. The computers at my residences in Freiburg and Bad Salzuflen had allowed for many online chats with friends and family. My room at Paderborn, Germany did not have internet access so I walked uptown again to this internet café. I heard about it through *The Torch*.

Tony Torchia, who walked alone to the café before I arrived, is a fellow Envoy with Major League Baseball International. I am told that he religiously heads to the computers each night to keep up to date with life back in the USA. He hunts and pecks on his keyboard a couple of cubicles away. After catching some news on the only English TV channel here—CNN, I watched dirt from today's efforts spiral down the shower drain and then headed here as well. I arrived haphazardly via directions offered by a German player who had attended our long session with the Deutsche Baseball Akademie. His English was poor—but good enough to get me here. I was pretty much lost the whole way . . . especially after the additional 'helpful' advice I received in broken English after popping in an out of stores to get back on track. I don't do well without GPS. I normally use landmarks, but so many buildings in Europe look the same: old.

Other than mealtimes, our days are filled with baseball, using the latest on-field training equipment and technology, from 9AM to 9PM. The DBA camps—developmental baseball programs sponsored by computer company Nixdorf—are led by Georg Bull and a qualified staff including German National team members, former US college players, MLB Envoys and the odd Dominican. Tony was here last week while I completed an Envoy assignment in Bad Salzuflen. This particular two-week DBA is held in the city of Paderborn, with facilities as good as any NCAA program. The caliber of instruction is very high. Chris Gannon, a former Boston College ballplayer, plays for the Paderborn Untouchables, who are in Germany's highest league. The Untouchables are a dominant force and have won the Bundesliga for years running. Chris assists at

DBA camps as does Mitch Franke. Mitch was the first player from the German Bundesliga to sign a contract with an MLB organization when he inked a deal with the Milwaukee Brewers back in 2000. There are other quality coaches here and we spend the majority of our days separately manning a station. Tony works mainly with hitting and I work one-on-one with the camp's catchers. A unique atmosphere—Dominican music blaring throughout the day—accompanies our training sessions, perhaps in tribute to the DBA camps held annually in Boca Chica. One of the coaches says it reinforces rhythm needed to play the game.

Tony is a bit of a mystery to me. I arrived in Paderborn the other day and other than brief interactions on the field we have not had the chance to *really* connect due our schedules. Martin Helmink, current coach of the Paderborn Untouchables, told me that in a book of baseball quotes pulled from his bookshelf the other night, Tony is listed saying, "Hitters are like snowflakes . . . no two are alike." I am familiar with this quote. Martin said underneath Tony's name: *Boston Red Sox*. I will have to prod Tony about that.

My time in the computer lab is wrapping up. I have fired off a mass email to interested friends and family updating them on my trip, sent a personal email to my wife, and checked the latest Toronto Blue Jays and Saskatchewan Roughriders scores. Smoke curls up from Tony's fat big-shot cigar as he looks down and squints, slowly searching for elusive letters on his keyboard. The tips of his fingers snap on the keys hitting them harder than necessary. I am reminded I am in Europe as his cigar is puffed in a public building.

Outside the accommodations for the Deutsche Baseball Akademie camp in Germany.

During our brief interactions yesterday, Tony suggested I may be crazy. Although that is not an entirely new occurrence for me, Tony's impressions are solely based on my first choice of assignment last year for MLB: Africa. Even more amazing to him was that I picked it over the more amicable Germany or Czech Republic. When Envoys initially meet each other, their first inquiries are often about the other coach's previous assignments. Tony, inquisitive of my African adventures, peppered me with questions before I could learn much about him.

We head out the door of the Internet café and begin the trek back to our rooms at Haus Paderborn, a college-dorm-style residence the entire DBA coaching staff and participants receive room and board at. Tony is over sixty and I am fascinated by his lengthy career in the sport. It is not every day you have the ear of someone who has coached in the pros, especially on a warm evening walk in a foreign country.

"Where's home for you Tony?"

"Arizona now, but I spent a lot of time living in Florida."

"What was your first taste of pro baseball?"

"It was over forty years ago." The end of his cigar burns red as he inhales and then sends a long stream of smoke outward. "I was signed by the L.A. Dodgers right out of high school in 1961. It's hard to believe it was that long ago. I was so excited that I spent my entire bonus in less than two months."

"What did you blow it on?"

"I bought a new Pontiac, an engagement ring, and some new barber chairs for my father's barber shop. In my first year, I made a whopping $250 a month playing in Keokuk, Iowa for the Dodgers. I was in *Dodgertown* at Vero Beach, Florida, that first spring for seven weeks . . . what a learning curve."

"Who was there?"

"Leo Durocher was one of the coaches. Duke Snider, Maury Wills, Roger Craig . . . I got to watch Sandy Koufax and Don Drysdale throwing on the side. I couldn't imagine facing those guys as a batter."

"I thought you were with the Boston Red Sox organization?"

"I spent my first year with the Dodgers. Things went well. I led the Midwest League in hitting with .338 and also RBI's with 94 . . . with only 10 homeruns, dreams of a triple crown were squashed. If you were not on a Major League roster back then you could be taken by another team after your first year. There was no amateur draft in those days. The Red Sox signed me during the winter of 1962 and I spent the next 24 years with them."

We turn a corner and our evening stroll darkens as the amber-lit lamp posts are less frequent than the previous street. Calm. Twinkling stars. It is an ideal night for a walk even though shops are *geschlossen* for the night. "How did your playing career wind down Tony?"

"I actually knew in my heart that I would never get a chance to play in the Big Leagues after my fifth year of pro ball. At 24, I won another batting title, this time in AA with the Pittsfield Red Sox. Two teams were added in the American League that winter and when nobody took me I knew the writing was on the wall. It was then that I first wanted to get into coaching. College baseball piqued my interest as I could coach and teach at the same time. I began classes to earn a Master's degree. I played another 9 years, mostly at AAA in Louisville and Pawtucket, attending school each winter in Boca Raton, Florida. I was an organizational player though."

The Torch's decades in baseball include a season with the Boston Red Sox.

"Good for an organization . . . but not good enough to make it to the Majors, eh?" I ask as we head down another long street. Not a single car, pedestrian or cyclist is in sight.

"Exactly. Being 5'10", 180 lbs. didn't allow me to show much power as a first baseman either. Maybe I would have made it as a catcher or second baseman. I got hits off of those top AAA pitchers so I knew I could get the job done. I never got the chance to prove it in the Majors though."

*　　　*　　　*

Tony inquires further about my trip to Africa last year as our walk continues. He laughs in disbelief when I tell him that I saw monkeys playing in the trees only a foul ball away from where we practiced. Wait a minute. I don't remember the last time we encountered anyone else on *any* street.

"Tony?"

"Yep."

"Where are we?"

Throughout our babbling, Tony was following me and I was following him. Now, neither one of us knows where we are or how to get back to Haus Paderborn.

"They are going to laugh tomorrow," Tony says. "I got lost by myself last week heading to the internet café. Here I am teaching 'the ways' to the new guy. Funny thing, when I was lost last time I asked for directions to where the Untouchables play and the guy said, 'Baseball Court?' I thought I was in business. Then, he promptly gave the wrong directions and I ended up more lost than ever."

Becoming lost doesn't bother me one bit . . .yet. I hope I am not annoying Tony with all of my questions. Interesting guy. I need to know more about his coaching days. We continue moving in the same direction, even though we could be actually heading the opposite direction of our waiting beds.

"When did you retire as a player?"

"1974."

"Guess what?" I ask with a grin.

"What?"

"That was the year I was born."

"Thanks for telling me that . . . it is always great to be reminded how old you *really* are."

"What was your first assignment coaching?"

"I coached with the 'Paw Sox' in 1975. Joe Morgan was the skipper. I then managed my own teams in Class A and AA for the next six years. My first team at Winston-Salem won the pennant. I became the third ever manager of the AAA Pawtucket Red Sox in 1983. I am told I am the only person to serve as a player, coach, and manager of the Paw Sox."

Unreal. Names of Boston players flash in my mind. Stars he attended Spring Training with, characters he grew to know on dugout benches, rookies he instructed, shenanigans behind the scenes. The stories! He would have interacted with some of the greatest Red Sox players spanning a generation.

"I spent 1985 in the Big Leagues. It was sweet."

I couldn't help but think of the 1986 World Series and Bill Buckner of Boston, who missed the ground ball at first base versus the New York Mets to lose the game. I realize he was not coaching in the Majors that year, but for some reason it jumped at me. Roger Clemens. He would've gave high-five to Clemens after one of the greatest pitchers of all-time struck out the side . . . and slapped Wade Boggs' ass after he cranked a homerun. Tony was fortunate enough to once call Fenway Park his *home field*. I feel like an eight-year old admiring a prof

We're lost. An awkward silence falls between us. Moments later, as if on cue, a car emerges from the darkness. A yellow light on the top of the roof, words sprawled in German, clues us in that it is a cab. Oddly, it nearly passes by us. Maybe the darkened streets shadowed our waving arms.

"Hey, we're lost. Can you take us to the baseball field . . . the one where the Untouchables play?" Tony fires off, talking out of the side of his mouth, stogie clenched between his teeth.

The Turkish driver speaks no English and either speaks no German or the little German I offer is tainted by my Canadian accent.

"Baseball Platz," Tony says, "Near the British Army Base. Bang-Bang!" he says, bringing his hands up, extending one of his arms to imitate a long gun, other hand pulling the trigger. The widened eyes of the cabbie make me wonder if he might speed off thinking he is about to be held up by two nut-jobs. It doesn't help that Tony is now swinging his hands like a bat, mispronouncing the German word for hitting. With a thumb gesture toward the back seat, the driver knows customers when he sees them. I realize we are no worse off and might see a familiar sight on the drive that we can use as a landmark. We need to get in the back. Besides, it's getting crisp out.

After riding in awkward silence for a few minutes I ask, "You know, I have heard your quote that 'hitters are like snowflakes'. That is so true."

"You know what's funny? The original quote was cut down a bit before it made it into the paper. What I said was, 'Hitters are like snowflakes . . . no two are alike . . . and when they face heat they both tend to melt'."

I have heard too many undecipherable conversations in German so I can appreciate how the driver of the cab must feel hearing us blabber in a language he doesn't understand. As Envoys, we are surrounded by conversations that simply sound like gibberish. It is nice to finally have it reversed.

German radio fills the conversation void for a while. Tony blurts, "Car driver! Who is a famous race car driver?"

"Jacques Villeneuve?" I offer.

"No, a German guy. Yeesh."

"Schumacher?"

"Schumacher Street. That is where the Haus Paderborn is," Tony says tapping the driver on the shoulder. "Schumacher. Schumacher Street."

"Schumacher Straße," the driver corrects. Street must be his only English word.

I have to ask Tony a personal question. It's bugging me. Our ride home will soon end our evening together.

"Doesn't it haunt you?"

"What?"

"The fact that you were so close to realizing the ultimate dream for a baseball player, playing AAA all those years, and were just shy of making it to *the Show*."

"Not really. It became easier to accept as the years passed. I made good money for the times in AAA and just loved to play. The feeling of hitting a ball perfect, making a solid play, knocking in a big run . . . AAA *was* my Big Leagues. Baseball has been good to me. I made it further than most. I have no regrets. You should feel fortunate too."

"About?"

"Are you kidding? You may not have played professionally, but you are traveling the world with baseball. You're spreading the game internationally with Major League Baseball. You've seen a lot too you know."

*   *   *

We are heading home. I am glad for this night. I think tomorrow I am going to ask Tony about what signals they use in the pros. Handing over some Euros to the cab driver I watch Tony slowly and painfully get out of the back seat.

"Are you okay? I didn't notice you in pain walking."

"Yah, it's all good. I slipped and fell on the field at Hunstetten last assignment. I had to go to the hospital and get my ribs checked out. I will be able to laugh about it sometime . . . but not yet. It hurts too much. But that's another story."

I bet it is. As we enter the main door we part company with a simple *Gute Nacht* and a chuckle. Tomorrow is another day.

I think I will learn a lot from this guy.

That winter I got an email from Tony. "Brent, you will never guess where I am." After hearing of my journeys in Africa and stating I was nuts, Tony informed me he was in Uganda and Ghana. On one of the trips he was accompanied by none other than Major Leaguers Dusty Baker, Reggie Smith, and Dave Winfield.

Through further email and phone contact, Tony told me his love of coaching had been rejuvenated. He spent six months of the year as a hitting coach in a Taiwanese professional league. I also found out that after his stint with Boston in the Big Leagues he coached and managed at the minor league level with the San Diego Padres, Colorado Rockies, Houston Astros and Montreal Expos organizations. I also learned that I had actually watched Tony coach—although I hadn't met him yet—when I attended Edmonton Trappers' games when they were in the AAA Pacific Coast League. I also found it pretty cool that years ago, in my first year of college baseball, I bought a minor league hat of the Ashville Tourists. It was my 'go to' hat at the time . . . Tony Torchia was actually their manager when I put it on my head that day all those years ago.

Arbeit Macht Frei
(Work Will Set You Free)

"My mother had a horrific life. At fourteen, she was in the Nazi concentration camps. Her sense about life now is, every day above ground is a good day."

—Gene Simmons

On an off-day from Envoy duties in Germany I toured Berlin and visited historical physical structures including the Reichstag, Olympic Stadium (where Jesse Owens won four gold medals in Nazi Germany), the Brandenburg Gates, Checkpoint Charlie and remnants of the Berlin Wall. My guide for the day emphasized the importance of educating others on German history. Through a simple question I was able visit a place I had wanted to see for myself since elementary school. Many trips on off-days during my travels have impacted me as have experiences on the field . . . but few lingered with me like Sachsenhausen did.

Where is the nearest concentration camp?
    This would be something his students back home could gain from: an actual visit to a camp by their teacher. Ever

interested in history, he was aware that the majority of concentration camps were located outside of Germany's borders.

Sachsenhausen. Near Oranienburg. It is about forty minutes by train.

What? Really?

Sure. Very close. It is in good shape too. It was built in the 1930s . . . about the same time Berlin hosted the Olympics.

At his residence that evening, he was told that an upcoming morning baseball camp had been postponed. Opportunity. He left at 7AM that Thursday for the train station and walked across remnants of the Berlin Wall, where the words *Berliner Mauer*, inscribed on brick countersunk to the ground, outlined the former barricade between East and West Germany. He bought a ticket at a kiosk and climbed the steps into the train. Forty minutes, alone, in silence. He turned his ear toward the speaker behind him and waited for the voice to break over the intercom. It was difficult to hear above the screech and scratch of the steel wheels on the tracks. He strained not to miss the recorded German voice—*Achtung: Oranienburg.* The train lurched to a stop. He got out, headed down steep cement steps and walked around the city for twenty minutes, an occasional detour into shops for directions. *Sachsenhausen?* They knew. They pointed which way. According to small street signs, he was going in the right direction and would soon arrive at his destination. A small, grey monument labeled *TODESMARSCH* was appropriately shaped like a tombstone: *DEATH MARCH. April, 1945.*

The lush flora, typical of Germany, contrasted with the simple, impenetrable concrete perimeter wall of the camp. He headed into the museum shop for literature—in

English—to guide his free walking tour. He grabbed an informational pamphlet. A lady came out from behind her glass desk and offered a handheld device the size of an old-style cell phone—*Set it to English immediately. Read the signs and push the buttons to match the code. A story will play for each building or monument. Please use it.*

A section of the Berlin Wall located at park in the city.

The diorama of the camp just outside the shop was as detailed as any model he had seen before. From his vantage point it looked like a large triangle. He turned into the street and walked down further. A sign pounded into the grass made it clear that he should punch in a code for the device he carried. Through the device he heard: *Down this street was where people got off at a former train stop and were pelted by bottles and rocks upon entering the camp.* An eerie calm. A large full color sign, hung on the grey stone of the perimeter wall: *60 Years Since Liberation.* Another, viewed as he neared the entrance, featured a man on the right side of the sign, aged sixty years since he was last at the camp—white hair matching his collared shirt, a stern facial expression and sad eyes. A horizontal band of a picture of Caucasian skin served as backdrop—*125422,* tattooed in blue ink, the seedy quality of one etched in the back of a garage. A small triangle was also inked below on the band. At the bottom, typed in white: *SIX NUMBERS, June 24, 1943.*

As he entered the gates with a left turn he saw a stately white building down the cobblestone path. *Station A. The entrance to the camp.* Cut into the metal bars were the words *Arbeit Macht Frei.* He learns it means *"Work will set you free."* From an SS man: *The only way to be free was to go out the smoke stacks of the ovens.* As he passed through the gates the roll call area came into view. A picture from a pamphlet showed some of the thousands who had been sandwiched in that very spot over sixty years ago. It was shaped in the form of a semi-circle and *was used as a torture area to instill obedience and fear.* Directly across from Station A was the former gallows, which in addition to dangling those killed, also *hung Christmas trees during the holidays of Hitler's reign.* An inner wall enclosed portions of the roll call area. A path like a track-and-field oval ran along the side of the wall, housing an area originally designed for shoe testing. *Prisoners, especially pink triangles (homosexuals) walked, sometimes for days, on a variety of surfaces including broken glass, testing the soles of ill-fitting army boots for the Nazi regime. Those exhausted from walking the track were beaten and, in some cases, shot.* He paused to reflect—as if at someone's grave.

He learned of the three-cornered design of the camp. Guard towers were strategically located at each point of the triangle, which allowed for *crossfire and the chance to eliminate prisoners from any vantage point within the walls.* A barbed wire fence, the Death Strip, remained—a barrier that prevented anyone from getting within fifteen feet of freedom. A kill zone for perched guards also served as a possible method of suicide for prisoners who could take no more.

He moved on. The Jewish barracks was now a makeshift museum but oddly showed remnants of a fire. He smelled burned wood. He was informed that *in September of 1992, only days after Israeli Prime Minister Jitzhak Rabin had visited, arsonists—right wing extremists—attempted to destroy the building.* It remained unrepaired. On the main floor of this building, the size of an average home, often had 400 prisoners squeezed into it. In a small partitioned room, only *8 to 10 people at a time would have been able to surround the circular fountain basins to urinate.* On the entrance wall, attached to the blistered paint and charred wood was a sign: *The washrooms were yet another site of terror, SS guards are known to have drowned prisoners in the basin for trying to wash their feet. The bathroom stalls housed a short row of toilet seats which were only to be used for a few minutes in the morning and evenings—those too old, sick or weak were trampled.*

He visited the cell block and prison yard—areas separated from the general compound during the war. The walls, adorned with the artwork of those who survived captivity, held framed portrayals—a testament to the horrors committed. Bare-chested prisoners depicted in white pants with blue stripes were shown tied with their hands bound above their heads, strapped to poles to be whipped and beaten in a

punishment known as *Pole Hanging*. Other art showed ema-
ciated victims bent over small tables to be struck in similar
fashion. He looked down the corridor and recalled a typical
prison scene from television—narrow halls and barred jail
rooms on both sides. In each cell was a black and white pho-
tograph of a former prisoner with their bio, a candle, and a
flower pot that rested on the floor against the back wall. He
exited at the far end of the hallway and saw that many of the
buildings had been removed or destroyed—only their foundations lingered. Three vertical poles, about eight feet high
and spaced four feet apart from each other, bordered green
grass in the courtyard. A bouquet of fresh roses rested at the
foot of the middle pole. As he neared, a picture flashed in his
head—one of three people nailed to crosses.

A portion of the area where the Nazi's conducted shoe testing experiments on
prisoners at the camp.

The white stone sniper towers jutted meters above the
reddish brick of the outer wall fortifying the stranglehold. It

was clear that no one could escape a bullet in the triangle of death outside. Thick green trees, taller than the watchtowers, surrounded the outside perimeter of the camp, deep and large enough in number to shroud the walls from view from other areas of the city. He saw a building down the path that appeared to be newer than the rest. He walked towards it and entered. A picture of Heinrich Himmler and his henchmen stood in contrast with the other displays. The Nazi was shown leaning forward like a curious child—surrounded by dozens of other soldiers. A propaganda picture showed an SS man happily passing a cigarette to a prisoner who was in the bottom of a trench. The man in the hole leaned on a shovel. *The snapshot was used to show dignitaries on the outside the positive relationships between soldiers and inmates at the supposed work camp.* Little did the captive know he was digging his own grave.

Large clumps of human hair in glass cases were accompanied by pictures that showed full barrels of locks that had been *cut from heads to control lice, and in* some cases, *used to fill mattresses and pillows.* Thousands of shoes rested in containers that stretched from floor to ceiling. An empty can the size of a large tin coffee container, pellets scattered about, was shown nearby: Zyklon-B. *It was used for the gas chambers.* A bunk bed was off to the side. He walked up and compared its small size to the art on the wall which portrayed eight people jammed to a bed, necks strained to poke out amidst the other pin-striped prisoner uniforms. Down further, he saw black-and-white pictures that included a noose that dangled from the gallows across from Station A and a prisoner stuck horizontal in the Death Strip. The barbed wire was clawed into his body as he dangled sideways. Dead.

Teeth. A hand, palm up in a picture, held dozens of teeth that had been scooped up from a plain, large barrel. *Nazis extracted them for their gold fillings. Some of it was made into jewelry.* Suitcases of dentures were evidence of the thousands upon thousands killed. Posters on the wall listed the countries of those persecuted.

He exited on the other side of the building, puffed his cheeks and exhaled a long, forced breath. A small bird chirped in a tree and broke the silence of his walk. He headed down a cobblestone path towards a slender vertical sculpture forty meters high. It was a monument known as *The Liberation] Memorial.* It was erected in 1961. On it, eighteen red triangles pointed downward from the top of the grayed cement of the structure. *They symbolized the political prisoners from eighteen countries held at Sachsenhausen.* He turned and noticed he was in a direct line across from the gallows. This was also directly across from the roll call area and Station A. Out of nowhere, a Japanese man approached—the first person he had seen for hours. A picture was needed. He got the man's attention, pointed at him and pulled out his camera. He pointed to himself and the background behind him. Positioned just to the left of the direct line, he made sure that Station A would be visible over his left shoulder. No smile.

He noticed that there was a break—an exit—in the wall. He walked towards it and left the triangular confines of the camp. Just outside he noticed planted trees and grass over unmarked mass graves. *These buildings nearby were for 'special prisoners' and remnants of a Soviet camp from after the war.* Part of the community of Oranienburg was within meters. Further on, countersunk at ground level, he found a trench large enough to drive vehicles into. Logs were tightly stacked horizontally to make side walls and one end wall. On one end of the structure—still below ground level—was a white wall with two brown doors. *This was an execution trench. Bullets were shot through holes in the doors and were absorbed by the logs if they passed through victims.*

Nearby, he saw a white walled structure that had a flat, tent-like roof. At its entrance on a separate concrete monument was inscribed: *DEN OPFERN DES KZ SACHSENHAUSEN. In Memory of the Victims of Sachsenhausen Concentration Camp 1936-1945. Station Z, a cynical reference on Station A. Prisoners entered through A and exited, skipping letters of the alphabet, exterminated here at Z: the gas chamber and crematorium. The SS also had mobile ovens to make murder more convenient.* A sign read: *The building, still wholly intact, was blown up by the KVP (Militarized People's Police) of the GDR (German Democratic Republic) in 1952 and 1953.*

He took off his hat, entered and saw the foundations that outlined the area for the ovens and chambers. On the floor of one area he saw what appeared to be the drain of a shower and also pipes with taps. Some of the doors of the crematorium remained intact. *Until early 1943, prisoners who were cremated were killed prior in the execution trench. Some also were brought to the crematorium after being hanged from the gallows or by death from camp maltreatment. For mass exterminations a special room was used in the infirmary. SS men dressed as doctors and told prisoners that they were going to routinely examine them—including measuring their height. Behind the height gage, in the wall, was a hole where other SS men put a gun through and shot the victim during measuring. Loud music was played to mask the gunfire. After March 1943, gas chambers and nerve gas were used in an effort to kill at a more rapid rate. Years after the camp was liberated, during excavations for restorations at Sachsenhausen, mass graves and ash were found.*

He entered the inner walls of Sachsenhausen again and walked down the side wall towards another point in the triangle. The Pathology Building. A pole shed attached to the side of the building served as a cover to the descent into the Mortuary Cellar—*storage for bodies prior to cremation.* He removed his hat again and walked into the building. Small rooms. Clean and bright with yellowed tile that began from the floor and went up the wall about five feet. Large cabinets were on the end wall of the room. Each one had glass cupboard doors. Directly in front of this area, an examination slab, tiled entirely in white. *Autopsies, tooth extractions, cruel experiments and other atrocities were performed* on those very tables. Again, he paused and gave a deep exhale. He turned a corner and walked downstairs. The room was cold and poorly lit. *During World War II, bodies were stacked in this morgue.* He did not stay long. Once outside again, he looked at the pole structure attached to the building and noticed that going down the steps, in the middle of the path, was a long conveyor belt.

A small building is located just outside the camp. In that very building, plans were hatched to carry out The Final Solution. Every concentration camp within the Nazi's grasp had ties to that building. Sachsenhausen was a model for other camps and was a meeting place where orders were issued to the other Nazi facilities of death. Its close proximity to Berlin allowed easy visitation by those in military hierarchy who wanted to witness in person the latest training that guards received and the latest barbaric techniques to control prisoners.

He walked toward the former Infirmary—now a museum—and another exhibit. Photographs on the wall displayed a number of stories of those persecuted. *Josef Schopper kept himself alive by playing a cherry wood colored guitar that was now on display behind glass. He used the instrument to entertain SS men even after being transferred to Auschwitz.*

He trudged on. He examined a wall that detailed the *Examinations of Sinti and Roma.* It displayed mannequin heads that hung to show *racial profiling used by the Nazi's included measurement of nose length, examination of the position of eyes on the face, degree of slope of the forehead, and type of chin. These assisted in the identification of race and people's supposed intelligence level.* Another exhibit showed charts and guides to skin, hair, and eye color. *These assisted the Nazis in the identification of those who were not Aryan and said to be racially inferior.*

Josef Schopper's life-saving guitar used to appease Nazi guards at the camp.

He shook his head and continued out the door. Station A was near. He had completed the triangular tour. Over the years he had always picked up a stone at historical and memorable sites he had visited around the world. They were for a rock fountain he had in the backyard of his home in Canada. He knew it was not right to take one from here. He had a lump in his throat. A number of tourists had gathered near the entrance of the camp. He asked one of them to take his picture just under the barred words *Arbeit Macht Frei*. He did not smile. Shadowed from the ceiling of the entrance of Station A, his face was obliterated and blackened. Unrecognizable—charred.

* * *

On a flight home from Europe—on another Envoy trip—he flipped through an in-flight magazine and read about a subtitled Austrian feature film that was based on actual events at Sachsenhausen. *The Counterfeiters portrayed the largest money counterfeiting operation in history—it was set up by the Nazi's through prisoner labor in the 30s.* That same year, an American feature film, Valkyrie (starring Tom Cruise), was released. *Some of the conspirators in the plot to assassinate Hitler were believed to have been taken to Sachsenhausen.*

I am not sure what it is about the haunting experience of walking the actual pathways of history that is so intriguing. It is more unsettling of course when those paths are ones where murders were carried out. I was once asked, "Why on earth would you have wanted to tour such a place where horrible acts were committed?" We must. I think we need to feel uncomfortable more often. We need to be reminded, and very bluntly so, of the absolute atrocities humans are capable of. The utopian belief that the world will forever be rid of them is seemingly erased daily with news of the evils of man. The mere hours I spent at Sachsenhausen continue to haunt me, but that is nothing but a paltry moment of pain . . . I cannot comprehend what life was like suffering there during its operation.

One thing about baseball is, it can certainly be an escape—a positive distraction from the frustrations, problems, and issues we deal with in our day-to-day lives. I have never pondered life at Sachsenhausen while on a ballfield . . . but the idea of Sachsenhausen has startled me awake in the middle of the night.

Out of His Left Mind

"Be who you are and say what you feel, because those who mind don't matter, and those who matter don't mind."

—Bernard M. Baruch

I became a fan of Bill Lee at a very young age when he pitched for the Montreal Expos. Even in my early years I could tell he was a character. Perhaps that was what drew me to him—or maybe it was his scruffy beard. I first met him at the American Baseball Coaches Association conference in Nashville, Tennessee. He was peddling bats. During that experience, later, when I spoke with him a few times by phone, and each and every time I saw interviews with him on the internet, he was and always will be, unapologetically: Bill Lee. I like that. Even though a person might not agree with everything he says he or she can still respect him for speaking his mind and staying true to himself.

Bill Lee is an eccentric former professional baseball player whose antics on the field and off have engrossed fans for decades. Crazy beards, defiance of marijuana laws, wearing a beanie with a propeller, and even donning a gas mask on the field all contributed to the legend of the man nicknamed *The*

One of the most colorful players to have ever appeared in Big League baseball.

Spaceman. A student of philosophy and mysticism, Lee has made his fair share of otherworldly comments. He offered on brain hemispheres, "You have a left and a right. The left side controls the right half of your body, and the right side controls the left half. Therefore, lefthanders are the only people in their right mind."

The early part of his career predates my birth. From 1979 to 1982 though, I knew him as the quirky lefthander who occasionally threw that big lollipop lob pitch to another favorite Expo—Montreal catcher Gary Carter. Leephus. Spaceball. Part cartoon character part intense competitor, Bill Lee was a successful pitcher whose free-spirited antics often overshadowed his ability as a player. Lee won a College World Series while playing for the University of Southern California and had three consecutive 17-win seasons with the Boston Red Sox. He made the All Star team in 1973. Later in his career, Lee butted heads with manager Don Zimmer, whom he likened to a gerbil, and was shipped to the Montreal Expos at the end of 1978. His career in Major League Baseball ended in 1982 after he was released for protesting what he thought was mistreatment of teammate Rodney Scott.

In a phone call with me, Lee offered, "I took my uniform that night and ripped it in half. I draped it over Jim Fanning's desk and wrote a note informing the manager that I was AWOL: *Went to the bar. If you want to, come and get me."* Lee never appeared in the Big Leagues again.

Blackballed, Lee continued to play the game he loved. Anywhere. Everywhere. World-wide. I first met him while I was travelling as a MLB Envoy Coach. I had a blog section on my website called *Have Glove Will Travel.* Someone in Lee's camp came across it after googling reviews on Bill Lee's new book which coincidentally had the same title as my blog. The man emailed me, complimented me on my posts, and suggested Bill Lee come out to Saskatchewan to play baseball sometime. That winter at the American Baseball Coaches Association convention in Nashville, Tennessee, I met up with Lee at a booth where he was promoting a Canadian baseball bat company. We talked a bit and shared stories about baseball in far off locales and around the world.

When his book became available in Canada I ordered it and learned of something else about him that piqued my interest—his brief 'political career.' I guess we had another thing in common in addition to our passions for baseball and travel: we both had agreed to run in a political election that we had no chance of winning.

I ran for Member of the Legislative Assembly for the provincial Liberal party when they were on 'life support' in Saskatchewan in 2007. They had pretty much been that way for decades. Not having a single MLA represent the party going into the election certainly didn't help. A dominant force in the early part of the province's history, the party had pretty much dropped off of the political landscape by 1975, save a time as Official Opposition in 1995. My great grandfather Arnold was the Humboldt MLA for a term beginning in 1948 when they were still relevant. I felt a bit of a duty to be the standard-bearer for the Liberals in the constituency and knew that it would be the only time I could run before they grew even more irrelevant on the provincial scene and also before my wife and I started a family. Call me crazy, but I enjoyed the election, even though I had zero chance of winning. I truly did 'take one for the team.' Bill Lee's candidacy in 1988 was even more implausible. Ridiculous, actually. Bill Lee thought big . . . he ran for *President of the United States.* Well, sort of. He ran on a Canadian ticket. The Rhinoceros Party of Canada was a satirical organization making a mockery of federal elections for decades following its inception in 1963. When asked about the aims or goals his candidate would work towards upon election Rhino founder Jacques Ferron said, "The same as yours—nothing!"

Past campaign promises of the Rhinoceros Party of Canada had included:

- Repealing the law of gravity
- Providing higher education by building taller schools
- Ending crime by abolishing all laws
- Putting the national debt on a credit card
- Changing currency to bubble gum, so it could be inflated or deflated at will
- If they somehow won an election, they would immediately dissolve and force a second election

One candidate—upon receiving free television air time offered to political parties—stated: "I have but two things to say to you: celery and sidewalk." In 1988, the Rhinoceros Party ran a candidate named John Turner in the same riding as the Federal Liberal Leader, former Prime Minister John Turner. Some were not amused—especially when some Rhinos finished second in their ridings in Canada. The party was squeezed out entirely the next election in 1993—their last federally—when new rules made it mandatory for Canadian parties to have a candidate in at least fifty ridings with a cost of $1000 each.

Bill Lee's run was ludicrous—as intended. When I talked with him he reminisced that he had wanted Hunter S. Thompson as his running mate, saying, "Who knew more about vice in America?" Lee's platform included banning guns and butter since "they both kill" and he now claims that had he been elected, a team from the Dubai would be in the American League East. He said he was first approached to run by Charlie McKenzie, the head of the Rhinoceros Party in Quebec at the time, and agreed to participate as he was told he was "guaranteed to win." Donors to his campaign were limited to giving a maximum amount of twenty five cents since "we thought it was a two-bit office anyways."

Lee, of course, did not win. In fact, he was not even permitted on the ballot. Surprise. He may have upset some people for lampooning the political process—others perhaps applauded him for it. If there is one thing Bill Lee gets across in the clips I have viewed, articles I have read, and my interviews with him, it's his desire to shake things up a bit, stand up for what he believes, and protest when he thinks he was been crossed—shaken with humor and stirred with gonzo. He certainly is his own man and his enthusiasm to connect with others and interact with people is infectious.

"If I accomplished anything as a player, I hope it's that I proved you could exist as a dual personality in the game. I was gawked at every time I stepped on a diamond," he said during a phone interview. "Away from the ballpark, I wasn't concerned with getting ahead of anyone. On the mound, I was always out to win, but I hope I showed people that game is indeed a game and that it shouldn't be taken too seriously. It is meant to be enjoyed. All fun aside . . . I would still take you out at second if the game was on the line though."

The *Wrong Stuff*, an independent movie based on a chapter of Bill's memoir of the same name, managed to secure the acting talents of fan Josh Duhamel. Ghostbuster Ron Shelton also stars. The film is set in the 80s and is about the demise of Bill's Major League career and blacklisting. It was directed by Brett Rapkin who co-produced a 2006 documentary called *Spaceman: A Baseball Odyssey.*

Ultimately, Bill Lee came to the realization he could basically play anywhere in the world except in the Major Leagues. He continues to travel with baseball and likely will until he utters his last impromptu remark. He is the oldest pitcher to win a professional baseball game. His passion for the game is only matched by his strong will and individuality, that make him one of the most memorable characters to step onto a big league baseball field. When I think of him I am reminded of a quote by Satchel Paige: "Age is a case of mind over matter. If you don't mind, it don't matter."

Africa Diary - Uganda

"The most important things in life aren't things"

—Anthony J. D'Angelo

I will never, EVER let a baseball player back home complain about his equipment. Paul caught in our scrimmage today with a decripit mask that most North American kids would have likely thrown in the dumpster. The foam pieces looked like a cat had nibbled on them. The flimsy chest protector offered little more protection than a sweatshirt. His barefoot squat behind home plate also bothered me, mainly because it was normal to all the players that someone could play baseball without shoes. I chose a three-country tour in the continent of Africa for my first MLB Envoy assignment, thinking it would be the place I would be least likely to travel to on my own. I knew it would give me a different perspective on things. That turned out to be the understatement of my life.

The diary that follows is from my first summer trip as an MLB Envoy. I had been offered my choice of assignments: Germany, the Czech Republic or a three-country-tour of Africa that

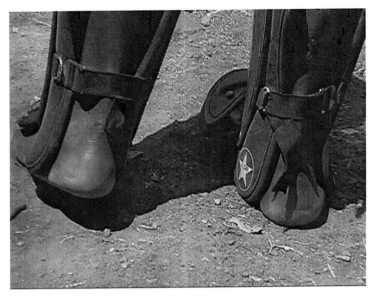

A barefoot catcher in Africa prepares to squat for the next pitch.

included Nigeria, Uganda and Zimbabwe. Nigeria had been cancelled only two weeks prior to departure—perhaps due to the travel advisory on the World Health Organization's website that blinked *POLIO OUTBREAK*. I had received several immunizations for the trip and had taken daily pills to guard against Malaria. South Africa, to be added in Nigeria's place, had been dropped since the timeframe to finalize everything was too short.

My mom had suggested that I keep a journal, as details, schedules, and incidents can be fleeting. A blog had been my first choice of recording my thoughts and experiences, but I was uncertain what internet access would be like. I left Saskatoon for Toronto and then went on to Chicago to join another MLB Envoy, Rusty Tiedemann. I knew little about him other than that he was a fellow teacher, from

Wisconsin, and his first assignment had been last year in Germany.

UGANDA

The itinerary to get to Africa was as complicated as it was long. Starting from Saskatoon, Saskatchwan, then on to Toronto, Chicago, and then London, England. From the UK I then went to Alexandria Egypt, to Addis Ababa, Ethiopia, to Nairobi Kenya, and finally to Kampala Uganda. In Ethiopia we learned our flight to Kenya had left already, which resulted in a lengthy delay. Somewhere along the way my luggage got left behind, leaving me with only my carry-on bag that contained some books, a toothbrush, my glasses and extra contact lenses, an mp3 player, and a notebook for diary entries. My cash and passport were strapped to my body with a money belt.

*   *   *

1:25AM in Ethiopia. We had been stuck at Addis Ababa Bole Airport for hours, the better part of a day blown after frustrations with British Airways regarding our delay. After I sipped on a Coke—the iconic label now in Amharic—the process of getting visas had begun. The moment we passed through the airport's exit doors, purchased visas in hand, we were quickly surrounded by about 10 Ethiopians who screamed and pointed emphatically in our direction—I couldn't help but think at the time that it was "game over" for us. Rusty, and an accidental travel companion named Patrick who latched onto us from Uganda, were as lost as I was trying to understand what was going on. One of the men from the crowd stepped away and had begun to shout back at the group. He turned, and in broken English explained that an *auction* was in progress. After a short time, one man had won out, and the others, despite being disappointed, helped gather Rusty's luggage and our carry-on baggage and put them on the roof of the cabbie's small, elderly Toyota. The remaining men opened the doors like chauffeurs—the lowest bid drove us to the hotel—$5.

The ride to the hotel—which had a British Airways office in it —was an introduction to what was in store for us. The streets were crammed with people who sat, laid down, walked and generally milled about. Guns were everywhere—alarming for someone who only had seen guns (in public) holstered on the hip of a polite RCMP officer. I managed to sneak a photo of a man in fatigues holding an AK-47 while he talked and shared a smile with a young girl. Pedestrians came up to peek in our window, some with an extended hand, palm up, and others making eating gestures with an imaginary fork. Patrick told to us to never open the windows and always keep our doors locked. He also said that some of them were "working."

*　　　*　　　*

11PM local. It didn't take long for us to nod off from the exhaustion of our travels. Eventually we were awakened from our sleep in the ritzy confines at The Hilton-Addis Ababa by a phone call from Pat Doyle, our MLB supervisor, who was working in the Netherlands. After hearing our predicament, Pat offered to notify my wife Melissa about my delay and see what he could do for us on his end.

*   *   *

I awoke early that morning to an indecipherable song and chant that came from a loudspeaker somewhere in the city. Patrick informed me that it was a Muslim call to prayer. The hypnotic hymn blended high-to-low held notes with a burst of words that sounded like an auctioneer to me. He said it was a summoning, five times a day, for mandatory prayer. We had ordered room service that night and had cracked the seal on the fully-stocked hotel room bar fridge—making the morning come that much more quickly.

*   *   *

3:26PM: We arrived in Nairobi, Kenya after we had met with British Airways at the Hilton in Ethiopia that morning and settled our dispute. My luggage finally had been located but *still* remained at London Heathrow Airport. Officials said it would be transported on the next flight out and would eventually arrive at the Entebbe airport in Uganda. They told me to stop at a desk at the Addis Ababa airport and I would receive money for incidentals from having lost luggage (which became 900 Ethiopian Birr—about $100 US).

*   *   *

Entebbe is in the southern hemisphere while Kampala was 20 minutes down the road in the northern. Not everyone can say they crossed the equator during their commute. The nighttime cab ride to our hotel was absolutely terrifying. The speed we travelled surely exceeded any limit, and as we weaved through traffic, the car alternated from one side of the road to the other. Apparently, in Uganda we were supposed to be *on the left*. The blur out the window was thousands of people milling along the side of the road in the dead of night. Many shops were still open; dead animals hung from hooks outside the premises. I write this in our hotel room—owned by the head of the Ugandan Baseball Association—glad to be in bed, but overtired and in need of sleep. I had known little about Kampala other than it was the country's capital and approached 1.5 million residents. Uganda's total population, nearly 26 million, was flooded with refugees from surrounding countries. I had researched the country on the CIA website—prior to leaving Canada and was shocked to have read that the life expectancy for Ugandans is 44.88 years. Less than 45 years?

I was able to telephone Melissa and left a message that I had arrived and was *safe*. Rusty was in a separate room down the hall.

*   *   *

I wanted to kill the birds outside my window. They squawked all night, and coupled with the heat in my room, made sleeping a great challenge. It probably also had to do with jetlag since we were eight hours ahead of North American time. I attempted to shoo some of the birds away from my window and noticed a bunch of cardboard, garbage and clothes below—a family was living in squalor between our hotel and the next building.

*   *   *

I plugged my electric shaver into my trusty power adapter; the problem was it was just that, an adapter, not a *converter*. Zap.

*   *   *

The veranda of the hotel was where I captured my first videos of Kampala. I panned left to right, and then, after I heard voices below, pointed my camera downward. On the ground below was a man who struggled to move forward as he pulled himself with his arms—legs gone from some unknown horrific injury. He looked up at that very moment and his face instantly turned to rage. I believed he thought I was filming solely *him*. As I pulled out of his view, my face reddened, chin dropped and eyes stared blankly at the floor. He screamed at me as I sheepishly made my way back to my room.

*   *   *

Overall, the day was quite productive. Breakfast had begun with the freshest fruit I had ever tasted in my life: watermelon, pineapple, pompey, and mini-bananas. I am not a pineapple eater, but those pineapple slices tasted like candy. We were offered an odd-smelling tea muddied with a milky substance that laid atop the water. Rusty and I opted out of and never even sampled it. I will try almost everything once, but I had read in the handouts from the Travel Clinic to avoid liquids that may have been made made from local tap water, are not capped, or are not seen being prepared under a rolling boil. We washed down breakfast with two cold Cokes that satisfied us not only due to the heat, but because they were in glass bottles—something I had not seen in years. Our backs had become damp with sweat even though we were wearing t-shirts and shorts, yet all the people walking around on the streets (and in the hotel) were fully clothed—some with long sleeves, and *all* with long pants.

Because we were delayed—after the missed flight to Kenya—the coaches were unaware we had arrived in Kampala. Due to our unexpected tardiness, Rusty and I wanted to make up time and be on the ball diamonds immediately. Eventually a practice session at a local University was hastily organized with fifteen members of a girls' softball team. Baseball-only

A wind-up game, not far from the Equator, after a long session at Sharing Youth Center.

facilities did not exist in Kampala; it was played on make-shift diamonds utilizing soccer pitches, cricket fields and the inside of track-and-field ovals.

Kaddu, in his early twenties, accompanied us and planned to continue to grow the game with his new coaching knowledge after we were gone. He was very passionate about base-ball and went out of his way to help us. Rusty and I agreed

that Kaddu was one of those types of people who were simply
a friend you had just not gotten around to meeting until now.
I had given Kaddu an MLB t-shirt as a gift and was surprised
to see him immediately take off the shirt he was wearing and
slip into the one I had given him. "In Africa, we don't save
things. You never know what can happen to you."

We had met another friend—after dinner that night—who
was to be our driver throughout our stay. Alex, a friendly
young man, had an infectious smile and laugh. Later that
day, he took us to a bank to exchange money--$50 American
became 90,000 Ugandan Shillings. Even though all our
expenses were covered on Envoy trips, I checked to see what
an average meal cost: 4500 UGS.

*   *   *

The equator intersects the northern tip of Lake Victoria. I was
told that the sun rises at 7AM and sets at 7PM—year round—
and that the average temperature was basically 30 degrees
Celsius (86 Fahrenheit) during the day . . . year round. Yet it
seemed hotter than the 30° I had been used to at home. I am
told that there were two dry seasons in Uganda during the
year and we were in one—strange to me considering I was
told to expect torrential rains occasionally. Uganda borders
with Kenya, Rwanda, Tanzania, Sudan, and the Democratic
Republic of the Congo.

Today was spent at a secondary school with a student
population of over 2000; those who came for our instruction
ranged 12 to 18 years of age. There were no windows in most
schools, just angled slats in the wall that allowed sunlight
to peer in between 8AM and 5PM. We worked with a teacher

named Jonathon and his PE class and ran drills and taught skills on a soccer pitch; the ground resembled the color of red shale. Some there said that the earth was "stained red from the bloodshed of Africa's grisly history." A teacher told us of the murderous reign of Idi Amin, "The Ugandan Butcher." Rusty and I didn't understand the come-and-go nature of Jonathon's class as the numbers of participants had fluctuated moment-to-moment. By the time we got to our wrap-up game, 45 students had become involved. Organized chaos . . . but fun nonetheless. Many students off to the side fiddled with baseballs and rolled them about with their feet. A number of them would cycle the ball with one foot and brace it with the other ankle to pop it into the air for a version of hacky sack. The control they had was astounding. It was especially impressive when they would gather in a circle and pass the ball with ease using their instep. It was a natural segue into an introduction of the pre-game baseball staple: Flips.

It was intriguing to see how interested people were in simply handling equipment for the first time. The limited supply that was available was greeted with such eagerness it brought me back to my first interactions with 'real' equipment. I had slept with my goalie equipment when I first got it as a young kid. The difference was that before I got my own, I had witnessed the various items utilized properly in person or on TV. Here, a student putting a glove on his head was not uncommon.

After we finished our sessions, we toured the school since we had an hour before we were to be picked up. Overlooking the field where we had demonstrated the game of baseball a short time earlier, we now saw hundreds of students engaged in a variety of activities. Some played soccer, or hacky sacked anything they could get their feet on; others carried school books wrapped in twine and tucked under an arm, or dribbled and shot baskets with worn out basketballs. It was a stark contrast to North American schools where, unless extra-curricular activities or in an afterschool program was going on, the grounds cleared out quickly after dismissal. It was clear that for many here playing in the school yard was solace from troubles they encountered in life; it helped them cope.

As we continued our tour of the school that day and headed into an Art room, I couldn't help but ask, "Kids painted these?" Most of the artwork on the walls were *very* detailed nudes, some of which portrayed rituals that involved knives. It was explained that one of the paintings depicted young adults "going to the bushes" for the male circumcision ritual. "They drink a wine made from berries . . . and then they dance." If what I saw portrayed was true, I bet they danced. I wonder what would happen if an Art teacher hung pictures like that at school back home?

We were drawn into a hallway towards another room by the sound of beautiful a cappella music, first thought to be an entire choir, but revealed to be only three people singing the melodic hymn. We headed to the parking lot, where I began to become very concerned. It wasn't because our driver was nowhere to be found o'clock. It was because of *the bee*. A large one had stung me and taken a chunk out of the web between my thumb and index finger on my left hand, and then literally peered up at me, released my numbed skin, dropped to the ground, and died. My mind swarmed with thoughts of that African bee. Great. Unsure of where we were exactly, with a driver who was hours late, in a foreign country with substandard medical services, I was standing there, bitten by a bee the size of a sparrow, with a stinger that pulled out like a wooden sliver.

*   *   *

Happy to report that I didn't croak. My hand puffed up and looked like it had a pocket of air trapped underneath where I had been bitten. Ice and time would take care of it . . . so I was told. The fact I wasn't teased for overreacting with worry perhaps proved it had had the potential for serious consequences. But what did I know?

Actually, based on my short stay in Uganda so far, I did know the following:

- Everyone seemed young . . . I really didn't see any elderly people at all
- AK 47s were everywhere . . . and I never got used to them
- It was plus 30 degrees out . . . and I had spotted maybe five people wearing shorts so far
- Generally, people I saw were sharply dressed . . . then again, considering I wore the same clothes every day and washed them in the sink (as my luggage was still missing!), my fashion barometer may have been off a bit
- Fruit was available everywhere, was cheap, and tasted fantastic

- I encountered only the most polite people who seem filled with faith
- People claimed they love Canada and Canadians . . . but they couldn't convey why
- I saw every level in the economic hierarchy
- I had been asked if I was a US Marine, American Soldier or CIA agent a half dozen times . . . funny at first, but it contributed to my wearing a baseball hat *all the time* to cover my shaved, bald head
- Rusty and I had farted often, without known cause and without scent. We had no idea why, and it was continuous for the first week. Altitude? I can't speak for Rusty but I had found it somewhat entertaining
- I craved laundered clothes

*   *   *

Slept like a corpse. My hand still had hurt from the bee sting but I never brought it up as I didn't want to sound like a sissy. A passerby noticed my puffed hand and said, "Be thankful it was not your face or forearm." It was so hot in my room I had to wipe sweat from under my eyes, and if I leaned my bald head over to the side, sweat slipped off and trickled down my neck to my shoulder. Could've been worse . . . Rusty said the bugs had their way with him each and every night.

*   *   *

After breakfast, I had gone to the British Airways office, a small room downtown, and inquired about my luggage. I was informed it still hadn't left London. They claimed it would arrive at the end of that week.

*   *   *

The morning was spent at Sharing Youth Center, a school where impoverished kids and orphans learned skills to ply a trade; it was sponsored by donations from a church parish back in the United States. Traditional school subjects were not heavily emphasized there. A child, eager to meet me came up and offered, "Sas-catch-ah-wanna- is in the province called Canadian Prairie. It is near Albammia and wheat growing is carried out on a large scale." Another student, a 13-year-old named Paul, caught my attention for other reasons: his imposing size and strong arm. He threw lasers down to second base.

I will never, EVER let a baseball player back home complain about his equipment. Paul caught in our scrimmage today with a decripit mask that most North American kids would have likely thrown in the dumpster. The foam pieces looked like a cat had nibbled on them. The flimsy chest protector offered little more protection than a sweatshirt. His barefoot squat behind home plate also bothered me, mainly because it was normal to all the players that someone could play baseball without shoes. I kept thinking how a player with his ability in North America would likely be nurtured and developed and have every opportunity, while Paul would linger in Uganda, far beyond the baseball fringes.

Later, we were treated to a tasty snack made from fried flour and eggs and washed down with warm bottles of pop that players sipped as though it was champagne celebrating their greatest victory.

Rusty and I stared off into space when the participants circled us, dropped to their knees, and offered a prayer to God, thanking *Him* for bringing us to Africa and helping them learn the great game. Goodness. What affect would we have on these athletes who perhaps had more pressing issues to contend with than learning the game of baseball? A distraction from the hard times they encounter on a daily basis? I commented to Kaddu that I had never worked with a more captive audience during clinics. He offered, "You bring them hope of an opportunity with the game." I had thought we should have brought more shoes.

$$*\qquad*\qquad*$$

We introduced a pre-game routine to a group of older players at one session and taught them cut offs and relays. I had intentionally overshot a fly ball to left with my outfield fungo bat in an attempt to knock some bananas off the trees that made up the natural fence of the field. I never dreamed I would ever see a banana plant fence at a ballpark, but since the opportunity presented itself to hit a ball into one, I couldn't pass up the chance. The outfielder retrieved the ball from the fruit forest as if nothing happened and fired it in to his waiting relay man.

After the session I went out and retrieved some of the bananas I had knocked down, came back, and started to eat one. I was scolded by a player—not for having knocked the food out of the tree—but for how I had pulled the peel back and had eaten the fruit. At home, I routinely snap open

An African player listens attentively to a throwing exercise.

a banana from the top, pull each peel down half-way until I have three sections, then snap off the fruit with my fingers and plop it in my mouth. I pull the three strands down to the base of the banana and pluck the last part of white mush out and eat it. I am left with nothing but a peel. I was instructed by a participant that, "Bananas are gifts from God, given to us so we can have safe food in the worst conditions."

He showed me how to *respectfully* eat it. He opened the top of the fruit, pulled the peel down a short way, bit off a piece, pulled down again, ate a bit more of the fruit, pulled the peel down further and then munched the last bit of banana and plopped it in his mouth so that only the peel ever came into contact with his hands. "You should never touch the fruit itself," he offered. "Your hands could have germs." I never looked at a banana the same way again. I wonder what other inadvertent disrespect I had shown in Africa?

*   *   *

The trip back to our hotel was mayhem. The traffic had been unbelievable. Decrepit bikes, cars and vans over-packed with people, pedestrians ... everywhere. The street was congested, had no traffic lights, and people tried to cut in as they nudged bumper-to-bumper. Halted vehicles snapped their horns like a pack of dogs barking at each other. Utter chaos to Rusty and me, but seemingly routine for everyone else.

*   *   *

While at a vehicle checkpoint on our way to another community, our driver stated, "I wish you didn't have a camera here. Don't let them see it." Immediately I stashed it under me and sat on it like it was an egg. I listened to the conversation—in Lugandan—that our driver had with the soldier. I had no idea what was said, but the glare Rusty and I received through the window worried me even more. I was relieved when the disdain of the person in army fatigues seemed to turn into intimidation by *our* presence in the vehicle. I later learned that people were often detained if they even attempted to take photographs of anything military. Our chauffeur, retired pro soccer player Barnnabus, explained, "They will smash cameras and then they smash you." I had overheard about the *force* that military people used. Lesson learned.

I was told, after we drove away, why we couldn't stray too far away from the city of Kampala during our time in this part of Africa. In Northern Uganda people feared for their very lives. The Lord's Resistance Army, led by Joseph Kony, a self-proclaimed spokesperson of God, charged his 'Kony

Rebels' against the government and Ugandan President Museveni. The recruits for his army: abducted children. Barely double digits in age, tens of thousands in number, they were brainwashed and taught to kill, maim, and torture with Kony and his henchmen. They hid in the bushes. All of this—according to Joseph Kony—in the name of the Ten Commandments. The signature torture was the cutting off of lips, ears, and tips of noses. I was numb. I couldn't help but wonder why I wasn't in the midst of a cavalcade of U.N. forces. We were mere hours away from these atrocities. How had I never heard of *this* before? The invisible had become clear.

*   *   *

I dug through the mass of papers printed off about Uganda (for my trip) and had found some references of the LRA that detailed their mass murder and abductions. I gasped when I read: *There have been periodic bomb attacks at various public places in Kampala.*

*   *   *

My exposed skin had been constantly slathered with sun block. I reeked of it. I periodically left my hat off each day so that sun rays didn't etch a tan line of 'ring around the skull' on my shaved head. The heat was scorching—like opening an oven door to snag a piping hot pizza without first letting the oven's heat escape slowly. The wall of heat was so hot, it felt like it could blister your skin . . . yet for me, now after all this time here, it felt, oddly, somewhat bearable. The sun had seemed to beam straight down like it was pounding the top of my cap and shoulders more intensely than the back of my legs. Oddly enough, my legs never burned in Africa.

I had refused our bottled water that was delivered to the field. When it first arrived I thought *Where the heck did they even get it?* My ignorance showed often. I had felt guilty that the players did not have any for themselves, so despite the heat, I told organizers I didn't need water anymore. How do you split a couple of bottles of water with 30-40 people?

*   *   *

Another group of kids had never seen an actual base-ball before. Again, the initial reaction was to kick the ball with their feet and hacky it up-and-down like a soccer ball. Keeping a soccer ball up in the air with the inside of your foot was one thing—but a baseball one-tenth the size? I had invited a few participants to a 'keep-it-up contest.' The winner received the baseball to keep. A young man kicked the ball up over *100* consecutive times before it was miscued and rolled in the dirt. When I asked how he had become so good he nonchalantly offered, "Lots of fruit . . . lots of time." In college we used to have *real* hacky sacks—knitted two inch bags filled with sand—to pass time before the rest of our teammates arrived for practice. I had always kept one in my ball bag since then. I left it for the players at that stop to enjoy after we departed.

*   *   *

On this day, as we unpacked our equipment, knowing smiles were shared between Rusty and me. We had dropped our bats and wiffle balls onto the ground and our eyes had become fixed on the group of players warming up on the side. Someone had coached them before. A smattering of mismatched uniforms. They partnered off, slowly spread out, and played long toss with a throwing routine. There were logical progressions and decent mechanics. We were pumped. Rusty went into some advanced infield drills and I worked with some pitchers and catchers off to the side. We were impressed by this group. Rusty and I had asked each other if they simply *appeared* strong in comparison to other unpolished athletes we had worked with, or if they were legit baseball prospects.

One guy especially stuck out: was it because he was 5'7" and the only one in a full baseball uniform? Another player had thrown gas. We didn't have a radar gun so I went

A practice session at a cricket oval with monkeys in the trees overlooking the play.

behind the catcher during a pitching workout—I estimated he touched 90 mph. I then caught him myself and, being a catcher who had caught everything from puss to pills, felt confident in my estimate. He was also an outfielder, had a hose for an arm, and ran effortlessly. Another—an unorthodox pitcher—had thrown bullets that brought muffled yelps from the catcher—perhaps due to the condition of his glove, which had as much padding as about three pieces of paper.

By the end of the day we had identified three prospects— all under 19. We submitted Player Identification forms on them. Part of our role as Envoys was to identify players who had professional potential. These players had made the grade and would be invited to Major League Baseball's Italian Academy for international prospects.

In this part of Africa, few fields are dedicated strictly to baseball.

*   *   *

I had been able, after days of trying, to finally send an email. Trips to the internet café were not as easy as I had hoped. It was located within a couple of blocks of our hotel but was usually closed by the time we were finished for the day. The computers there were slow and often froze up. I typed as fast I could and hit *send* frequently in hopes that even part of my messages would get through. I copied and pasted each paragraph as I progressed since I had lost a couple of pages of work during one visit to the café. Melissa told me that a cousin wondered, "If he is a teacher, how come he has such poor spelling in his emails?" I guess for someone unaware of my predicament, the thought was valid. I typ as fst as I can and watevr is wrten, is writtn.

*   *   *

We had spent a lot of time in one particular area that was actually a cricket oval surrounded by a 'track.' Kyambogo Cricket Oval. At one end of the field were a couple of huts where a family lived and some equipment was stored. The man who lived there periodically lined the track with a contraption that left a slick trail of motor oil that identified the lanes for runners to run in. He wore faded purple pants, a white tattered shirt, and had sleeves rolled up to the elbows.

His wife, head tightly wrapped in cloth, hung their unmentionables on the laundry line near where she tended to her outdoor cooking. Our temporary mesh net backstop was placed in the corner of our makeshift park near their home. I had asked repeatedly for us to move it to a less dangerous location in an effort to avoid any injuries. "This is where it always goes. It is best," I was informed. I shook my head when a foul tip smashed into the side of their clay hut—a chunk of their house laid on the ground as a reminder. The lady picked up the ball and tossed it, wrong foot forward, and laughed as it landed mere feet from where she had thrown it. No big deal I guess—to them, but when a foul ball eventually ricocheted off the side of their *goat* and scattered nearby chickens like a fox was in their midst, I thought we had to relocate. Nope. Another ball was selected from the pile to be used. The foul ball was retrieved later after the goat settled down and was less rammy.

That park, surrounded by thick trees and brush, had a familiar scenic quality that made me feel I might simply disappear—like the ghosts in the corn field from the movie *Field of Dreams*—if I walked into it. I had been told that monkeys inhabited the trees and that ball games were often stopped for a while when the animals crossed the field to get to their only water supply—a small pond on the other side. My initial thought was that the guys were teasing me. Claims were also made that the reason the monkeys hung out, hidden deep in the trees, was to seek shade because it was so hot. Wasn't every day hot in Uganda though? I was also informed that monkeys were considered pests by some and routinely killed when they snacked on local banana supplies.

*   *   *

One night I visited with some of the hotel workers downstairs. They asked plenty of questions about Canada. We talked about 'pop' being soda and I was asked how 'shit' meant excrement yet also could be something good (as in 'good shit'). They also did not believe the high price of alcohol and cigarettes in Canada. Health care funded through taxes? Statements they had made about Canada: "most peaceful country on earth," "grows lots of wheat," "religious place," "good people there." I had attempted to explain the game of curling and drew it out on a napkin that night—I am not sure they were sold on it.

Towards the end of that evening I broke a local rule and chatted with an armed guard. He said he was 29, though he looked 15. I started to talk to him about his gun and in the process, quietly took his gun and held it. Rusty, who apparently also felt at ease with the guard, snapped a picture of the man and me—the gun clutched tightly in *my* hands. The guard quickly retrieved his weapon with a laugh after the photo was taken, not angry with us, but perhaps worried someone might have seen everything. I wasn't worried. His clip and gun were free of ammunition—no more dangerous at that moment, than a baseball bat . . . or so I thought?

*   *   *

I forgot to write about the beer. In the evenings, Rusty and I had paperwork to fill out to document where we were, what we did, and who we worked with. It had become our routine to work on those papers while we enjoyed the evening cool, over a few beers, on the hotel deck. I couldn't help but stare at the stars and think that it was about the only thing that my world at home had in common with Africa. Naturally, I had to switch to local beer. Just before finishing my second beer each night my left eye uncontrollably pulled inward as if to look at an imaginary fly on my nose. I was not drunk. It happened over the course of three sessions and at that point the novelty wore off and it became too weird . . . a beer had caused my eye to get a mind of its own.

*   *   *

I casually walked towards the internet café late one afternoon. A commotion caused me to spin around. I was 'greeted' by a uniformed man staring down a long rifle pointed at my head. The eyes that looked through the sites were bloodshot and full of hate and the tone of his foreign language alarmed me that I was in *trouble*. I froze. His tone became louder and more aggressive. I felt helpless. Then I heard, "Mzungu! Mzungu! Come here!" from a local across the street. I had edged a few feet back and the guard—dressed in navy blue— lowered his weapon, waved it out to the side and indicated I was free to go. I was frantic to cross the street to get to the man who had beckoned me from the other side. But the traffic, unregulated and busy as always, was too dangerous to cross. "Just come . . . they will stop! They *will* stop." I had no sooner put my foot out onto the street and the traffic halted. They waited as though they were at a train crossing back home. I briskly walked across towards him and, behind me, the traffic immediately resumed full-tilt as if it were simply a video game off of pause. "Do you realize that if you were me, you would have been shot, no question?" he asked. Apparently, I had passed in front of a bank and walked through the area where cash had been transported from the back of a plain-looking vehicle. How was I supposed to know? "You are lucky my friend," he said. "Usually first they shoot. Then they deal with the problem after." I assumed Mzungu meant 'white guy'. Maybe it meant *idiot*.

*   *   *

At one session a young boy started to scream after he slid into second base. His wrist was broken . . . for sure. I'm no doctor but I just knew it was. One of the adults off to the side nudged me away from tending to him, and after he retrieved a large, black carry bag, pulled out a white creamy substance and smeared it on the boy's wrist and arm. He then milked the injured area up and down. The sounds from the boy haunted me almost as much as his eyes: it was as though he knew this injury would affect him for the rest of his life.

*   *   *

During breaks, I had often visited with players and tried to get to know them better. One time, I asked the age of players I worked with—through the assistance of our translator. I was not prepared to see one of the kids come to tears. Our helper explained later that the child was orphaned at an early age and didn't even know his last name, let alone his birthday. I never asked that question again. A lot of children lost their parents due to AIDS. It made me think of the term *night commuter*—the tens of thousands of children in the north who flow into urban centers each evening after dark to seek refuge from LRA attacks, mutilations, abductions, and murder.

*   *   *

That night I listened to the Tragically Hip on my MP3 player, and by the third song tears streamed down the side of my face. I didn't bother to wipe them as they trickled onto my pillow. I had not cried since my dad died of a sudden illness two years ago . . . but as I lay in bed, I thought of a lot of things. I thought kids back home and how they seem to have everything they will *ever* need . . . and then some. I thought of the young boy's wrist injury and how easy it would have been to take him to a local hospital back home in Canada. I thought of the LRA. I thought of the bank incident and what could have come of it. I thought of the night commuters.

Our role had been to develop and promote the game of baseball. We were indeed doing that, but we couldn't escape what we encountered first hand in day-to-day life here. I thought of how grateful people had been when I had given out handfuls of Blue Jay bookmarks, Canada pins, and baseball cards. Pennies with the maple leaf on them were *cherished*. It overwhelmed me. I had broken. I needed to change. Somehow, I knew I had already, but it could never be enough. I could never do enough.

*　　　*　　　*

The urge to relieve myself had become unbearable during one practice session at Kyambogo. I had gone into the bush (past the hut where the family lived) and continued down the side of a little bank. While I took a leak, I heard the tree branches rustle. Something swished in the bushes in front of me. Monkeys! I panned my head on a swivel, looked for movement, and tried to catch a glimpse of the jumps. I rushed back to my ball bag and retrieved my video camera. The monkeys, light brown with tinges of green, were smaller than I had anticipated and reminded me of toy breed dogs. I started to call, "Monkey . . . monkey . . . monkey!"

I heard some giggles and looked back at a group of players who had assembled behind me. They smiled, happy that I had finally seen the monkeys and possibly satisfied that I knew that they hadn't lied to me about their presence in the trees. Suddenly, a commotion erupted up at the edge of the bank. I ran to investigate. The 'laundry mom' swatted fiercely at a stray dog with her broomstick—bowser had been after her chickens. She guided the birds to safety, and after she lashed the dog with a few sharp whips of a stick, effectively scared him off. I recalled thinking that there was no way I could've made up some of the things that happened near the ball fields on this trip.

*　　　*　　　*

The rest of my luggage had finally arrived. I had never wanted a stash of gitch and socks more in my entire life. After I had changed into a fresh set of clothes, we headed to a craft market. Rusty questioned my thinking as I bought African trinket after African trinket . . . but he later followed suit and also purchased plenty of affordable, unique gifts for those at home. I felt obligated to support local crafts-men, but also admired their work. I would have bought more stuff but there was only so much room in my luggage at the time—although ultimately, we gave away much of what we brought in our bags from North America and indeed had more space.

*　　　*　　　*

One day we travelled to the 'Source of the Nile River' at Jinja, Uganda. During sessions, curious young spectators on the side munched on freshly cut sugar canes. I eventually gnawed on a piece too. The memory of Dubble-Bubble gum came to mind—a gush of flavor followed (after a minute of chomping) by zero taste. Perhaps I should have sucked the flavor rather than chewed it out.

During one of the outfield drills—at Lugazi—I was unable to use my long fungo bat. I had to manually send the ball high in the air because: If the ball was hit in front of the players it stopped dead due to the knee high grass . . . throwing gave me more accuracy and a chance for them to catch the ball in the air. Motorcycles zipped by sporadically between the outfielders and me . . . and were often 20 feet in front of us. At least 100 onlookers milled around haphazardly on the field and I didn't want people to run into the holes that were on the playing surface or encounter the burning garbage, ant hills or swans (the size of ostriches) assembled nearby.

Funny thing was, I had heard someone compliment how great the field conditions were. It did actually have foul lines—marked typically with used motor oil. Rusty had pulled the long straw that day and had won the privilege to teach drills and hit grounders on the relatively forgiving flat surface of that infield.

On the highway back to Kampala—after we stopped for pineapple—I had noticed a boldly labeled, red and white Coke sign for a bottling plant off the side of the road. Really?? We had stopped at one of the numerous fruit stands nearby and stuffed the back of our vehicle until it was full of fruit. Before we drove away, pineapples were cut up for the ride home. It was the best fruit I had *ever* tasted. I thought of all the trouble and fuss that was likely encountered getting a Coke facility up and running in Uganda when in fact nothing, in my opinion, could top the taste of fresh African fruit.

Africa Diary - Zimbabwe

"We can complain because rose bushes have thorns, or rejoice because thorn bushes have roses."

—Abraham Lincoln

The next leg of that summer trip was to Zimbabwe. I couldn't help but think that a piece of me was staying behind in Uganda and that I had also snapped up a part of the people there as well. Zimbabwe would also soon win me over. Baseball people consistently have been some of the best I have ever encountered. Airline people, on the other hand . . .

ZIMBABWE

The sadness of leaving Uganda—our new friends and unique experiences—had been countered by anger when my emotions percolated at the check-in counter of the Entebbe airport prior to our departure. I was aware of airline guidelines and followed them: I triple-checked the weight of my luggage to ensure it was well under requirements. I had wanted to leave room for trinkets and souvenirs yet to be purchased in Zimbabwe, so altogether my luggage weighed less than

60 kilograms. At the counter though I was told I was only allowed *30 kilograms* total—or a sizable levy had to be paid. This was contrary to what was stated on my airline ticket print-off. The man at the counter emphasized that since I was on African soil and was to fly to another African country (without leaving the continent) I had broken the chain of my original international flight plan. He felt he was entitled to charge me $250 for the extra weight.

Another counter had opened up to avoid delay for other travelers while we dealt with the issue. I refused to pay this unjust amount. The agent was stunned when I opened up both of my bags and started to take things out. I rationalized what was essential for the rest of my trip and made piles of giveaway merchandise for unsuspecting people waiting to board other flights. There was no way I was going to be profited off of. Tourism booklets, souvenir pens, Ugandan food items (including chili sauce and coffee), extra contact lens solution and soap were all passed out to those interested. Rusty laughed about the soap. A friend of mine had recommended I bring plenty of scent-free soap since mosquitoes are often attracted to fragrances. Getting malaria was not part of my travel plans.

I also removed a bongo drum—carefully wrapped in clothing—that I had purchased from a street vendor, partially because the guy needed the money and also as a memento for my brother Brad back in Canada. I decided to carry that on. My bags—still overweight—had now only cost $40 USD in penalties. I fumed when I was not given a receipt. Time was at a premium and we didn't want to risk missing our flight, so we left.

The bongo drum did not delay us at security, but after boarding the plane, I realized it didn't fit it in the overhead bin. A friendly flight attendant offered to put it in her personal storage area, which also proved too small to accommodate the hard, wood drum. She then had suggested we move our seat location to an emergency exit where the bongo could fit, tucked under the seat in front. A colleague of hers chimed, "All exit areas must be free of all luggage or other obstructions." In the end, I flew south to Zimbabwe, via Kenya, in my regularly assigned seat—the drum partly underneath it with my feet and my knees pressed uncomfortably up towards my chin.

*   *   *

We were picked up by the President of Zimbabwe Baseball, Mandishona, and their National Team Manager, Yosuke, from the airport in Harare. The city appeared small in size—an illusion as there were 1.6 million living there (2.5 metro). We didn't stay in hotels during that assignment. We were house guests of a former Japanese minor leaguer Yosuke Murai, who headed quality control for a Japanese company based in Zimbabwe and big into baseball there. Yosuke insisted on this change of venue as he felt the location of our hotel was unsafe. His beautiful home had concrete walls that outlined the perimeter, military razor wire in place of ivy, locks on every door, vertical bars on every entrance and on *all* windows. A guard, armed with a baseball bat, popped out from behind the fence and moved behind our vehicle as we entered the electronic gate of his driveway. He slipped back into the yard, bat in hand, as the opaque gate snapped securely behind us. After we got out of the car, their three dogs gave 'friendly' chomps on our forearms like they were chew toys. Were they supposed to leave marks though?

The Murai's had servants. Their house and yard were immaculate and decorated with a species of greenery as foreign to me as the family's security measures. As we entered our guest house, I pondered how I would be able to get out in the event of a fire—bars on the windows? Each and every house we passed on our drive to their home appeared to also have the same precautionary measures. The line I had read from travel website Lonely Planet had said it all: **WARNING:** Currently, Zimbabwe is in a state of turmoil.

*   *   *

The Zimbabwe National Baseball Team refueled from their morning workouts with four slices of bread and a cup of water. It was evident that there was skill on the field, but arm strength, bat speed, and power could improve. Some quick runners though. In the mix of their lunch break I managed to record some players who chatted in their native languages, Shona and Ndebele; the latter showcased the fascinating click and clack sounds that was part of their pronunciations.

Dream Park was one of only a handful of fully developed baseball fields on the continent (along with ones in Nigeria and South Africa) and apparently, I was told, the first actual baseball park built in Africa. I had heard a lot of different claims over the course of my trip though. The playing surface of the field was substandard to anyone used to well-groomed facilities in urban North American areas ... but playable none-theless. The dugouts and backstop were better than most I had seen in a lot of small-town fields in Western Canada. The park was funded by Japanese donors as a gesture of good will. Two small brown sheds that resembled porta-potties were

Dream Field at Harare, Zimbabwe was funded largely through Japanese donations.

located on each side of the dugouts. The wire fence that connected them also served as a laundry line—another thing I had not seen at a ball diamond *anywhere.*

*　　*　　*

It had been hinted by locals that a three day in-service on our agenda would be less than enjoyable as our audience would be teachers. Both Rusty and I were teachers, so we were not sure what to make of that. It was for a school division in Harare. Sunrays slipped in through slits in the windowless wall of the dimly lit meeting room. Perhaps it had tricked our minds into thinking that the room was cooler than the 35°C (95°F) outside. Rusty and I had attempted to lighten the atmosphere by teasing each other before we attempted our task of high honor: To *introduce* the game of baseball to a group of teachers, who in turn would introduce it to scores of students.

Twenty-one primary-grade teachers attended the morning session while eighteen from secondary levels showed up in the afternoon. We had been told to expect *ten* in total. Even so, it was awesome to be a part of. Comedy routines could have been developed as we fielded questions about the 'obscure contest' called baseball where 3 strikes meant an out, 3 outs completed a half-inning, yet 4 balls made a walk; a ball was fair if it hit the *foul* line and a base was also awarded if you get hit by the ball—yet a hit was what happened when you reached base safely. The teachers, male and female, picked up bats and wielded them like swords. They giggled when they rounded the base paths and cheered teammates and opponents alike during our scrimmages—always Brent's Blue Jays versus Rusty's Brewers. It was magic. Three hours each session, nine hours with each group, resulted in one of my most rewarding and memorable experiences on a baseball diamond to date. Participants chose 'the course' as their professional development and received a credit or coaching certificate for attending. During each session we were pressed multiple times to give up of our hats, gloves, and 'special shoes.' Teachers.

*   *   *

We had had the chance to go downtown where my most prized purchase was a lump of elephant turd encased in a plop of clear glass—something I was sure Melissa would enjoy as paperweight on her desk at work . . . or not. I guess a Grade 7 boy might get a kick out of it on mine. The shop keepers were very aggressive, yet had been fun to deal with. Again, total strangers walked up to me and wanted to trade my shoes and hat for their African wares.

*　　　*　　　*

It was awkward and uncomfortable for me to find my shoes polished to a gleam by someone each and every morning, placed neatly beside freshly laundered clothes.

*　　　*　　　*

Communication home continued to frustrate me. I had tried to email my wife Melissa before bed one night, and in an hour and a half only managed to *read* four—unable to send a single one. She had tried to call too, but unfortunately we were out of the house each time. We had zero communication for over a week (though not for a lack of trying). I had wanted to tell her that I was a millionaire after I exchanged a couple of hundred American dollars for Zimbabwe currency.

*　　　*　　　*

I was past first base and down the right field foul line, nonchalantly hitting fly balls with my fungo bat to outfielders, when a player screamed, "Get down! Get down! Get down!" Before I could even bend my knees my catcher flattened me to the ground and held me down in the dirt, his palm pressed firmly in the small of my back. My first thought was to expect a hail of gunfire from an automatic weapon as we laid down there in a quasi-push-up, silent. In center field the outfielders maintained the same horizontal position. "What the hell is going on?" I whispered to the catcher. "Shhh . . . bees." Bees? A horrifying hum in the shape of a cloudy refrigerator approached. I had never laid so still in all my life. After passing the outfielders, the buzzing rectangle wove in our general direction, hovered a bit and then danced its way across the field. No one moved. Eventually the players stood up, nonchalantly dusted themselves off, and assumed the ready position for the next fly ball hit to them. It was as though nothing happened, which made the occurrence that much more unnerving to me.

*   *   *

We eventually found out why there was a laundry line outside the two sheds at the ball park: two players *lived* there. No bigger than an average garden shed back home, the 'homes' contained their personal belongings and the tools for their job of maintaining at the ball park. I think Yosuke paid those players himself to work there so they had some form of income.

*   *   *

After a string of standard sessions we happily had an unexpected and much needed day off. Mr. Murai (as his wife called him) took us uptown to tour the city and look for souvenirs. He insisted that we buy the claw of a lion. Being an idiot, I pictured a paw, cut off at the wrist joint, but in reality it was simply a large toenail. I didn't really care for one . . . yet still bought it. Yosuke said I would be crazy not to buy it considering it was worth 10-to-15 times the $40 USD I paid for it.

This lion was as intimidating in person as it appears in the picture.

Sure. In the afternoon that day we toured a couple of wilderness areas that had known populations of lions, giraffes, wild boar, warthogs, zebras, antelope, impala, and monkeys to name a few. A man delivered a dead cow, and from the safety of our vehicle we watched the lions tear it to ribbons. The lions were curious and came right up to our car and nudged and butted the tires with their heads.

Our next stop was to meet up with an old man who had assembled his own collection of traditional African wildlife—a ramshackle zoo. A tip at the end of our visit was the only payment necessary. The man had lizards, crocodiles and pythons, which were offered to us to pick up and hold as though they were cuddly kittens. The man lacked one of his arms. It had been cut off clean from his right shoulder. Despite envisioning the incident that had hacked his missing limb, I obliged and held a 10-foot-long python. He showed me how to approach and clutch it so I wouldn't be injured. I filmed the giant snake so Melissa would believe me when I came home. Later, I picked up a smaller snake and put it on my hat. It immediately coiled and tightened around my head. A split-second decision led me to fake that it had bitten me. I screamed out a quick yelp and everyone gasped and jumped back. The old man nearly had a heart attack. As payback, perhaps, I was later bitten by a lion cub in a foolish miscalculation of how close I could actually get to it. Strong jaws indeed. It didn't bleed as bad as the pain made me feel it should have. My favorite moment, though, was when I dumped a handful of salt-and-vinegar chips on a tree stump for a monkey that had chased me. Enticed, he gobbled them up, devouring them so quickly that his nose immediately ran.

*   *   *

One day, we spent 8:30AM to 5:30PM observing a primary and secondary tournament. I shuddered at the site of catchers and umpires behind home plate without masks. At one point, a youth player—in minimal catcher's gear—looked the other way as he talked to someone off on the side. His pitcher, in the midst of warm up pitches, tossed the ball and smoked the catcher right in the side of the head. I think it hurt him as bad as it sounded.

While waiting for one of the teams—an hour late to show up—I visited with players off to the side. I was roasting from the heat and asked another player his opinion of it. He heart-ily agreed. It was the first time I had heard a local complain about the temperature. I wonder if it had anything to do with the sweater and wool hat he was wearing at the time.

The enthusiasm and intensity level of the girls' softball games was unrivaled by anything I had ever seen. Anywhere. Ever. For every single pitch, swing, or foul ball there was a momentous eruption of noise—the *entire* game. I took it they didn't get to play many actual organized games there. The girls near the benches, who watched their teammates and peers battle on the field, chanted cheers, screamed at the top of their lungs and danced. Rusty and I pondered what was going on when a medley of English phrases broke out that included bars of "Happy Birthday." It was no one's birthday. It was strung together with miscellaneous American phrases for the American game, I guess. To our amusement infielders also had *yelled,* "Thank you customer!" and "We enjoy your business, come again!" after batters struck out or popped up. We heard this on every field, during every game, and it seemed acceptable ballpark chatter.

*   *   *

Yosuke, his wife Gisella, and their son Kim took us to a rocky wilderness area that exemplified Zimbabwe's nickname, "House of Stone." Rock formations seemed to defy gravity with their ability to stay balanced and even be walked on top of. After a long and strenuous vertical hike we came across a historical site that contained cave drawings said to be over 13,000 years old. A few years back, some lunatic had barged in and tried to spray-paint over it all, largely succeeding in his goal. What remained of the original, ancient scribbles was as haunting as it was impressive.

Later that afternoon we visited the 60,000 seat National Sports Stadium which served as a hub of activity for local cricket, soccer, and track. We met with a government official to discuss our stay in Zimbabwe and then waited for our ride back—which never did come. Eventually, we had to take an 'E-taxi' back into city-central. The vehicle was basically a late 1960s extended mini-van that seated nine to ten comfortably—trouble was, we had 22 passengers and one irate baby inside. Luckily, no chickens were inside, though I had seen that elsewhere a few times. We were stopped at a police checkpoint and I thought for sure that the driver was going to be ticketed for excess passengers or no seatbelts or something. Nope. The officer only checked that the driver was in possession of a valid license.

*   *   *

I had hidden a newspaper article from Melissa before I left Canada. A couple of days before my departure for Africa, I had read an article in the World in Brief section of the *Saskatoon Star-Phoenix* that detailed atrocities committed against white farmers as part of government efforts for land reform in Zimbabwe. Led by President Robert Mugabe, a 'movement' had begun over the last few years to redistribute land. What began as a 'willing seller, willing buyer' program had changed drastically. Property seizures. Violence.

*   *   *

We had been sent to do clinics, spread over the course a few days in Mutare, located minutes from the Mozambique border. In a move that puzzled us, we were sent by train rather than the two-and-a-half hour car ride. The train left at 9:30PM and did not arrive in Mutare until 6:30AM—*nine hours later!* I DID NOT SLEEP A WINK. The train jerked and swayed as I attempted rest in my 45-degree angled cot— my head banging on the bunk wall with each jolt. We seemed to stop every 10 minutes to exchange passengers. They yelled every word of their conversations over the noise of the loud train. It was *the* most brutal trip of my life. We checked into our hotel and then basically passed out from exhaustion.

After a few hours of slumber, we ate lunch and started a long day of sessions in Mutare. Eighty high-school-aged kids were there. Even though we had limited equipment, we managed to keep players active most of the time. Most wanted to hit or go after fly balls. Because so few could throw accurately, Rusty and I continued our iron man batting practice pitching. No L screen. Some of those comebackers really hurt. I couldn't help but think that had some of the players we worked with had better knowledge of the mechanics of the game at an earlier age, we would have found some gems out there.

We went to bed early that night—our weary bodies insisted. At around 3AM, I awoke to Rusty shouting, "I think I have lice!" He flicked on the lights, rushed to the bathroom and frantically scratched at his hair over the sink. He used both hands and every finger as he scrubbed his hair like he was using imaginary shampoo. Bugs. Hundreds of squirming little bugs landed in the porcelain sink below as he rubbed his head. I went over and pulled back his sheets and found an army of what looked to be ants. They had set up camp at the top of his bed, near his pillow. We slid his headboard from the wall and were shocked to see that the creatures had spilled through the electrical outlet behind his bed. Rusty was relieved he didn't have lice and I, for once, was happy I didn't have any hair.

Rusty stormed down to the hotel office and complained that he wanted alternative accommodations. When the man at the front desk came to investigate, we were startled to see that as he didn't understand, after he had cleaned up the area a bit, why we wouldn't want to remain in our current room. He seemed to see us as prima donnas or something. After he left, Rusty told me what a hassle it had been to even get the man to come to our room in the first place. When Rusty arrived at the front desk, he found the man sound asleep and snoring. Rusty said his head was resting on his folded arms and his loaded gun laid on the ledge in front of him. Rusty apparently stood back and called to him which brought no response. After repeated tries, he told me he had approached the man, knocked on his head like it was a locked door, and finally after a few attempts, the man awoke, perturbed that his sleep pattern had been broken. While he visited our room, his gun remained at his desk the entire time, unattended.

*　　　*　　　*

Our ball clinics were mainly at a school in Mutare. It had the same backdrop as when I pitched at an AAA Canadian Championship where I blew my shoulder, in Trail, British Columbia—beautiful blue sky, picturesque rolling hills, small mountains adorned with light shrubbery. Even though it looked cool I still felt a bit uncomfortable as it reminded me of that devastating experience. Our sessions that morning were to be with females, with the males following in the afternoon. We were told that there would be an ten to twenty participants maximum. Of course . . . 45 showed up. Rusty and I played the guessing game for the afternoon when we were told our turnout "should be twenty." Over 70 made

Working with large groups in a foreign country is especially challenging when there is a limited supply of equipment.

their way onto the field—all of various age and talent levels. The high turnout was problematical as we only had five bats, a dozen balls, and fifteen gloves to host sessions from 9AM to 4:30PM. We kept all of the kids busy though and used improvised drills and played modified versions of baseball to take advantage of the acres of field.

After one session we were offered African Tea—which instantly reminded me of the cloudy, smelly drink in Kampala. I politely opted for Coke which brought a raised eyebrow from one of the school administrators. I told him that I had stomach issues and couldn't handle drinking warm liquids. I didn't feel bad about saying that one bit.

Later, an invitation was extended to take us to a wildlife area where we were lucky enough to observe elephants, wildebeests, and even a rhino in their natural habitat.

*   *   *

We headed back to Harare via bus, which seemed like a strange way to go. It was an overly crowded, decrepit vehicle that reminded me of a Greyhound bus, and the bumpy road and poor shocks offered less-than-ideal conditions to write diary entries. I will never forget that bus ride. Every stop, people outside flocked up to our sweltering vehicle and tried to peddle their wares of fruit, beverages and candy, pestering us through the open windows. There was a comical rotation of unpleasant activities that went on:

- a chorus of babies cried (while others coughed, sounding like they were actually choking)
- A mentally challenged man in the rear of the bus continually hit himself in the face and intermittently screamed at the top of his lungs
- A visually imparied man walked up-and-down the hallway of the bus and 'sang' loudly off-key; he held out an upturned hat for donations and bus fare . . . the *entire* trip

To top that off, another bus in the fleet had caught fire ahead of us and half of its passengers were transferred onto ours. They squeezed in and sat on the floor until no more people could be wedged in—while rest waited for another vehicle to board.

I eventually found out why we had taken the bus back instead of the train. Yosuke was apologetic. He explained how he had wanted to drive us round-trip to Mutare, but his work schedule didn't allow it. Then, stone faced, he informed us that the morning after we arrived in Mutare the same train *derailed* just outside of Harare. Over 70 injured. Deaths. I cried behind my eyeballs.

*   *   *

We left Zimbabwe and flew to Johannesburg, South Africa. We were on our way home. It was only a short stop. We then boarded a twelve-hour flight to London, England, flew eight more hours to Chicago (where Rusty and I parted company) and then I traveled to Calgary. After a bit of a layover I had a short flight to Saskatoon and was then picked up by Melissa for the one-hour drive to Muenster. In many ways it was 'just like that and I was home' . . . I think for the most part because of the daze I was in from the most amazing trip of my life. I was home for only a week and then left for training camp with the Saskatchewan under-18 all-star team that I helped coach. That team flew to Thunder Bay, Ontario for the Baseball Canada Cup, thus completing basically an *entire* summer of baseball travel. My wife was not amused.

One more duty yet remained before I left Zimbabwe that final morning, though. After breakfast that day, I (along with Mandi from Zimbabwe Baseball) was interviewed on the Zimbabwe Broadcasting Corporation's nationwide program *This Morning.* Rusty had opted out for needed sleep. When we arrived at the gate of the television station we were met by a soldier, AK 47 in tow, who, after checking our identification, jogged beside us in a military march and escorted us to the studio. I am not sure if his purpose was to protect us or to *suspect* us. I had almost burst out laughing when, during our live interview on TV, a close-up showed up on one of the monitors—my name was totally misspelled and the word AMERICAN blinked repeatedly underneath it.

At the beginning of the African assignment I had wondered: what will stick out as the most outstanding highlight? Before the adventure I had been a novice traveler. Now I had flown 56 hours on fourteen different flights through nine countries, traversed three continents and had travelled over 24,000 miles (38,000 kilometers) on a single trip. Rusty and I had reached over 1100 players, teachers, coaches and administrators during our stay. Upon my return to Canada, I knew it was impossible to narrow it down to one. The entire trip was the highlight.

If one word could summarize how the trips to Uganda and Zimbabwe changed me it would be: perspective. Even though years have passed I often feel its influence. In my elementary school classroom students were engaged whenever I introduced my trip into certain units where appropriate . . .so much so that they collected school supplies to send with a local man, Norman Duerr, who was making a good-will trip to Tanzania. Another year we helped raise funds to help him transport a shipping container that he was organizing. The entire area helped to fill it with useful items. When I taught an English class later at a high school, my trips found their way into a novel study. Students again were captivated . . . but did we do enough? During a Media Studies class we were analyzing various newscasts when the Kony2012 videos were making their way across the world. Clictivism was rampant. Well-meaning individuals 'liked' something with their computer mouse and felt they had done their job. I told the students that what was occurring there in fact was not a new thing in many parts of the world and that in a month or so, after the initial shock wore off, the international news buzz on it would pass. It did. Anyone follow it a year later?

My ears perked up during the 2011 Little League World Series when I learned that a team from Kampala had earned the right to attend but could not due to visa issues. The next year, a team from Lugazi won out as well, had their visas cleared, and became the first team from Africa to attend the competition in its entire history. A team from Langley, British Columbia who attended the 2011 Series at Williamsport arranged a trip to play the Kampala team that was unable to take part. The Canadian team travelled to Africa to do so. A documentary was filmed and when it aired I saw familiar faces and coaches from my Uganda trip.

This whole visa and proper documentation kerfuffle was not foreign to me as I almost had a couple of players we found during 2004 trip snagged up by a Div. 1 JUCO in Florida. Passport issues. One of the players had indeed thrown 90 MPH when assessed by MLB scouts at the European Academy in Italy. Had I done enough? Will I do enough? Can we do enough?

Following Terry Puhl

"The secret to success is to do the common things uncommonly well."

—John D. Rockefeller

When I was a youngster, Terry Puhl was the only active Saskatchewan-born player in Major League Baseball. It would be decades later before another person from my home province would make the Big Leagues. Fewer than ten in total have had the honor to represent Saskatchewan. The number of Canadians playing in the Majors increases each year . . . as does the variety of ways in which to follow them.

1991. On the 29th of May that year, Terry Puhl appeared in his last game as a Major League ballplayer. It wouldn't be until August 6, 2013 that the eighth Saskatchewan-born player would appear in the Big Leagues. World class hockey players are mined regularly from the Prairie province, yet prospecting Saskatchewan diamonds to unearth that rare gem of a baseball player is a struggle. The over twenty-year gap from Puhl's retirement to Andrew Albers' debut allowed for a whole new way to engage as a fan in the 21st century.

In Puhl's case, his pro baseball career seeded when the Cincinnati Reds showed interest in his raw talent at age 15. A couple of years later, while playing with his hometown of Melville, his pro career budded after playing in the National Midget Championships held in Barrhead, Alberta. "We ended up winning the tournament and I was named the MVP," said Puhl. "The Houston Astros had a scout there, Wayne Morgan, and he asked if I was interested in signing a pro contract. He said he would venture down to Melville in a couple of weeks to put me through a workout. Two weeks to the day Wayne was sitting in our kitchen when I got home from school. He immediately took me to the local diamond and threw me from right field, ran me . . . and then informed me he wished to sign me," he said.

Terry Puhl is the most accomplished Saskatchewan player at the Big League level.

Puhl was on the fast track with the Astros and was playing AAA at 19. He made his Major League debut on July 12, 1977 and never appeared in the minors again. At the time, two other Saskatchewan born players, Dave Pagan and Reggie Cleveland, were on MLB rosters—an unheard of total for the Western Canadian province. Puhl was named to the National League All-Star team the following year and his superlative defense made him a lock in the outfield; his .993 career fielding percentage still ranks high on the all-time list for MLB outfielders. Puhl's career path was an anomaly for Saskatchewan ballplayers. Nowadays, most who show pro baseball potential initially toil in American colleges, and the few who are drafted and signed enter the lowest of minor leagues before being dismissed somewhere along their ascent to the Show.

Most sports in Canada struggle to snag the best athletes available—many of whom are filled with dreams of playing professional hockey. Having players from your vicinity reach the highest of leagues makes the dream more plausible for everyone else. The NBA's popularity was augmented in Germany by Dirk Nowitzki's stardom, and also in Canada with Rick Nash's prowess; specific sports programs benefit when their elite athletes qualify for the Olympics and bring heightened awareness to their activity. The profile of baseball in Canada was elevated when the Blue Jays won the World Series in 1992 and 1993, and continues to grow as each year more and more Canadians appear in Major League Baseball.

Saskatchewan Baseball's High Performance Director was asked prior to Albers' climb, *What would an MLB player from Saskatchewan do for recruitment and retention of baseball players in the province?* "It might have some impact," said Greg Brons, "Players in Saskatchewan may think, 'Hey, why not me?' As a kid I was an avid baseball card collector—any time I saw Terry in the pack I was pretty happy to see *"Born: Melville, SK."* Talented baseball players have come out of Saskatchewan, but with a provincial population that hovers around one million, there are simply less of them to pluck.

There is no easy road to The Show and there are many challenges to overcome. Saskatchewan's long winter brings with it a short season and infamously fickle weather can cause all too frequent game and practice cancellations. "I played baseball three months of the year; hardly anywhere close to my American peers (while growing up)," Puhl said. Having to squeeze a year's competitive phase within the window of May to August is a challenge others don't face in more balmy locales. As an association, Saskatchewan Baseball has made strides over the years to extend the baseball season and develop those deemed potential prospects with pre- and post-season camps and trips to the United States. Baseball Academies are now offered through high schools. Brons offered, "It is a very hard game to play. A person has to have a tremendous amount of coordination in order to be successful in baseball and many players don't have the patience it takes to develop those skills. Furthermore, with our short season those skills don't get fully developed."

One could ponder if a stellar hockey goalie from Houston would get the same number of looks from scouts as they would if they were blocking shots in Saskatoon, and on the flip side, where that netminder would regularly face more quality competition to truly measure their talent level. There are players all over the world who are underexposed, but no matter where anyone lives, the tools and skill set must be present, identified, and developed in order for athletes to reach their fullest potential. Players can't be just good . . . they need to be exceptional and be exceptional against top-level competition.

After Terry Puhl, Saskatchewan baseball fans were ravenous waiting for a homegrown player to finally have another MLB at bat or offer a pitch to the plate in the highest of pro leagues. Decades passed. Players from other Canadian provinces made it to the Majors. Regina's Dustin Molleken was poised to become 'the one' for Saskatchewan. He had played for Team Saskatchewan in his high school years and was originally drafted by the Pittsburgh Pirates in 2003; the 6-foot-4 right hander reached the highest level of minor league baseball and was a call-up away from ending the drought of a Saskatchewan player in the Majors. A 2012 attendee of the Colorado Rockies at spring training, Molleken pitched for the Colorado Springs Sky Sox, the AAA affiliate of the Colorado Rockies, before signing to play in Japan with the Nippon-Ham Fighters.

Then came Andrew Albers. The Team Saskatchewan southpaw from North Battleford earned a scholarship at the University of Kentucky and was drafted by both Milwaukee and San Diego, contributed to Canadian National Team victories, only to be later released by the Padres after having Tommy John surgery. Albers toiled in the independent Can-Am Association and had various tryouts for Big League clubs, eventually enduring a 32- hour car ride to Ft. Myers from Phoenix for a chance to throw in front of Minnesota Twins scouts.

"There was a lot riding on it." Albers wrote in a blog entry. "I knew that if it didn't work out, my career in affiliated baseball would probably be over. I figured I would play one more year in Independent ball and probably go to the real world after that." Then came his seemingly meteoric rise to fame. In two years Albers shot from A-ball to the AAA All Star Game, was named the Twins' Minor League Pitcher of the Year, and received his eventual late-season call up by the Twins. The wait was over. In his first two starts he dominated, with two wins and recording all but two of the 54 outs. He would end up with 10 appearances with Minnesota and a 2-5 record in the fall of 2013. Suddenly, a lot of people in Saskatchewan realized that they were Twins fans and the trek to the Twin-Cities somehow seemed a lot shorter.

Hailing from North Battleford, Andrew Albers broke the over two-decade drought of a Saskatchewan player making it to the Majors.

In the off-season, Albers' story of adversity and perseverance drew hoards of media interviews. He spoke at many a banquet, and he took part in a cross-province tour giving clinics and motivational talks—in addition to substitute teaching at his alma mater in North Battleford. Over the following winter some moves by the Twins led to Albers signing with the Hanwha Eagles of the Korea Baseball Organization (KBO). After a year there he was signed by the Toronto Blue Jays with an invite to Spring Training; Dustin Molleken signed a similar minor league deal just prior to that with Cleveland. Albers was the Opening Day starter at AAA Buffalo and has appeared with the Blue Jays in 2015.

Experiencing the debut of Albers in 2013 was simple for fanatics compared with Puhl's early playing days—the bulk of which occurred in the pre-internet 1970s and 80s. "Friends and family kept track of me through *The Sporting News* while I was in the minor leagues. The *Melville Advance* ran a special following of me on a weekly basis. My parents also subscribed to the *Houston Post*," Puhl offered. Times have certainly changed since then, when past-tense updates were the accepted norm for those out of state. Live Satellite TV and radio packages now broadcast every game of every team, pitch-by-pitch action is available on smartphones, internet sites host clips and condensed games, people can DVR events to watch at a later date, and with the instant nature of tweets and Facebook posts, even the most casual of fans can stay on top of things with little effort. Quite a difference from a few decades ago, circling a few trite descriptions of exploits with a ballpoint pen in week- old newspapers. Albers was texting many family and friends back in Saskatchewan on the day of his debut; condensed HD video clips of those game highlights were available within minutes after the game through MLB Extra Innings or MLB.TV for those who didn't follow it live.

Baseball players from Saskatchewan who aspire to play Major League Baseball have some struggles ahead of them . . . as do others with similar goals across the country and indeed the world. It is only a matter of time for 'the next one' to appear. Making it to the Bigs requires tremendous talent coupled with opportunity. Staying there is even harder, and will become even more difficult as the talent pool continues to grow. But following that standout's career, conversely, will become easier and easier as time goes on.

Long Toss

"Pizza makes me think that anything is possible."

—Henry Rollins

I travelled to Sweden my third summer as an MLB Envoy. I was recovering from shoulder surgery and bought a glove for my right hand at a thrift store and learned how to throw as a lefty so I could do demos. I really didn't have to ever throw much farther than fifty feet for my first clinics and for batting practice I moved the L screen up closer to the hitter or had someone else throw. I rehabbed my right arm on occasion and was throwing lightly with my regular throwing arm by the middle of the trip. Sound far-fetched? Wait until you hear about Philippe's story.

My eating habits while visiting countries overseas continue to be a juxtaposition: Japanese food in Africa, Turkish doner kebab in Germany, and now pizza at this Iranian restaurant in Sweden. Our lunch break from the Rattvik Butchers Basebollskola allows us to partake in this basement eatery downtown, owned and operated by the relatives of Robin

Hakimi—an Iranian born ballplayer participating in our baseball school this week. The more I travelled with baseball the more in my face it was that I was working with kids across the globe. Robin loved the game. Loved it. I think it is cool that an Iranian was introduced to an American pastime in Sweden. One thing that was never lost on me is how many of these kids have never seen a professional game . . . in person or even on television. You would think one of the best ways to grasp the true complexities of any game would be to watch it played by the best there is. MLB's work with online telecasts has helped in this regard. Even so, there is no substitute for people in person making a difference. Philippe Longchamps is one of those people.

Philippe casts a similar glint as I off the top of his frequently-shaved head. And he loves stories . . . hearing them and sharing them. He is a fellow Canadian, fresh off his marriage to a local Swedish girl, plays on the local adult team, and has been a more than capable translator for the youth camps recently provided. Philippe has more in common with me than our passion for baseball. He is a fellow teacher, and as I just learned, also yearns for international travel. Our conversation evolves naturally from the game we love to travel abroad. He is not an Envoy, and he inquires about my baseball excursions, with a special interest in my tales of Africa. Eventually our conversation makes its way back to him.

Philippe's French Canadian accent abounds as he chides, "I think it has always kinda been my destiny to travel abroad. I left Canada at eighteen and within five years I had been to fifty-two countries." The Iranian waiter brings him a Pepsi; a Coke arrives for me as we skim the menu.

Philippe Longchamps, a proud Expos fan, around the age when he tossed his bottle into Baie Trinite.

"You must have a few stories from your travels too?" I ask.

"Actually, my most amazing story is from when I was a boy in Canada," he smiles, "but you may have trouble believing it as it quite bizarre."

"Do tell."

"I had just finished Grade 7. It was 1988. I was going on a fishing trip at my cousin Pascal's family's cottage during summer vacation at Sept-Iles near Baie Comeau, Quebec."

The little French I know kicks in and renames the place Seven Islands—near the community where the Prime Minster of the late 80s, Brian Mulroney, was born.

"Baie Trinite is where the St. Lawrence starts. Pascal and I were very bored that grey, windy day and were inside listening to the Montreal Expos' game on the radio. They were playing the Reds. We sipped Pepsi out of those small glass bottles they used to come in—you know, the ones with metal twisty caps that you could screw back on and finish your cola later. I leaned over to my cousin and asked, 'Why don't we write a message, put it into these bottles and send them into the sea?'"

Cliché. But was it? As a prairie boy—a flatlander—throwing a bottle with a message in it was not something I ever thought about as a youth. My toss in a body of water in my home province of Saskatchewan, with over 100,000 lakes, would likely have made its final resting place at a cabin at a Regional Park ten minutes after I threw it in.

"Pascal and I wrote two messages each that day . . . and both were bilingual—good ol' Canadians I guess. Mine read:

HI, MY NAME IS PHILIPPE LONGCHAMPS. I AM 13 YEARS OLD. I AM FROM SHERBROOKE, QUEBEC, CANADA. I PITCHED THIS BOTTLE INTO THE ST. LAWRENCE RIVER ON JULY 21, 1988. I LIKE MUSIC. I LIKE SPORTS. PLEASE, IF YOU FIND THIS BOTTLE, SEND ME A POSTCARD AT THIS ADDRESS:

PHILIPPE LONGCHAMPS
4591 MON HAVRE
ROCK FOREST, QUEBEC
J0B 2J0

PS: PUT THE MESSAGE BACK IN THE BOTTLE WITH YOUR ADDRESS AND THEN PITCH IT BACK IN THE WATER PLEASE.

"So you had four Pepsi bottles total. All four bottles contained a message written in French and in English. Two bottles Pascal—two bottles Philippe?"

"Correct. Oh, and it was funny too as I remember we didn't even clean them. We took our last gulps out of the second bottles, quickly scrawled the notes, and then squeezed them in the Pepsis . . . the film of soft drink still inside. I did something else too though. I had a couple of packs of baseball cards along. I cracked them open and after chewing the pink stick of gum that came with it, I took it and pasted it around the inside of the bottle cap. You know, the threads of the bottle? Then I screwed the cap on. I can still see the gum jamming and sealing the space."

"You thought of that? How did that come to you?"

"Not sure. I think it was because of the idea of a metal lid. You know, salt water, rust. I don't know. But only *I* did the gum trick. Pascal didn't do that to his bottle. I don't remember if I even told him that I had done it. Being competitive I guess I needed an edge to make sure my bottle had the best shot at surviving the water. Anyways, we listened to the remainder of the game which our idol, Dennis Martinez, got the win in, and then went to shore and pitched the bottles like our hero 'El Presidente' as far as we could into the water. Prior to coming there we could smell cooking salmon so we quickly went back to eat. To be honest we never really thought of the bottles again."

My first bites of pizza are very good but the story has my full attention. As we continue to eat, Philippe relays that his stay at Sept-Iles eventually came to an end and he returned to his home in Rock Forest, a suburb of Sherbrooke. Toward the end of that summer, August 15, 1988, he was shocked to receive a postcard from a lady named R. Poulin who, on vacation about 100 kilometers from Sept-Iles, found one of his bottles. She opened it, added a message of her own, sealed it and pitched it back in the water as requested in the note.

"That is unreal! It actually made it that far. What are the chances?"

Philippe looks at me and says with a wink, "That was *one* of the bottles. The one she tossed is still out there with her accompanying message . . . but another bottle showed up too."

"Pascal's?"

"Nope. He batted 0 for 2. My average was a perfect 1.000."

My head swam with thoughts of the next bottle. Did it make it out of Quebec? How long did it travel before it was found? Where was it ultimately discovered?

As though reading my thoughts Philippe continued like a good joke teller about to deliver his punch line: "Put it this way, an Oceanographer on Radio-Canada attempted to study the path of the bottle and felt that it had to have become trapped in ice . . . spending a winter in the St. Lawrence Gulf before inching its way trans-Atlantic towards Europe. It was not found until the summer of 1992 . . . I was in Grade 11. It took four years and one day to be found."

I leaned forward, expressionless. My body language must have communicated some doubt about all of this as Philippe began rattling off the list of local, provincial and national media outlets that inquired about his story that year, including CBC Midday. I had no reason to believe that he was full of it . . . but the story was getting a bit outlandish.

In 1992, Philippe Longchamps left his home in Quebec with $3500, a backpack, a tent, and a fascination for the world. He flew to Europe, and after a month in Southern France picking grapes, was contacted by his mother back in Canada, first by phone and then with a letter containing more details. He was informed that some strange hoax was going on and that a letter from Ireland had reached his family in Sherbrooke with their *old* postal code on it—surprising in itself as it had changed to a new one a few years back. 'Some boy' claimed to have found a bottle that Philippe had sent four years earlier and now wanted to make contact and perhaps arrange a visit sometime."

Philippe went on to explain that he didn't think he had told his mom about the day they threw the messages into the water so she had good reason to be confused. He admitted he had not thought about the bottles again until that moment. Amazed, he wrote a letter to the address in Ireland and explained he was on a tight budget, was going to travel Europe as much as he could, but that his final duty before returning to Canada was to visit the boy and his family . . . but that it would take some time.

Together after an exhibition game for the Rattvik Butchers in Sweden.

"So I did. It took me eleven months to finally get there. I kept the letter in my backpack and with no advance warning I showed up on their door step in Ireland. I think it was June of 93'. I looked like a long-haired hippy . . .and likely had the smell to match."

"Where in Ireland?"

"Derry. It is in Northern Ireland. It gets better though . . . he was a *she*."

A toothy grin wraps my face, an eyebrow raised as I recall Philippe was delayed a few days for the baseball camp we are putting on in Rattvik—having just gotten married within the last couple of weeks. Why did they wait so long to get hitched? I couldn't help but think that this tale was something I could only have read about or watched in some movie.

"It's not what you think," he laughed. I went up to the house and knocked on the door and said, 'I am the guy from the bottle.' I wanted to say I was from Canada but was nervous and that's what popped out. A thirteen-year-old girl in a school girl outfit came to the door, followed by her brother, sister and mother. The girl's name was Erin so I guess that is maybe why my mother thought she was a boy."

Philippe entered the home, where they made their way to the living room and visited. Eventually they all went upstairs to the room, where the bottle stood upright on a desk. The bottle had transformed a bit and was now warped and polished in spots, the soft drink logo and paper inside faded by the sun.

"It was amazing. I couldn't believe it. When I put the bottle to my nose I could still smell whiffs of the bubble gum. I also couldn't believe how poor my handwriting was . . . but I guess I *was* only just out of Grade 7 at the time."

He recalled the girl being somewhat apologetic as she " . . . didn't do like he said and throw the bottle back into the water." She claimed she wanted proof she found something so extraordinary. "I'm glad she kept the bottle as evidence as nobody would have believed our story if she hadn't!"

"I have to ask you. Is your new wife her sister then?" I knew I should shut up in case that was the kicker and I just ruined his story.

"No," he said with a chuckle. "The sister was actually younger yet." The girl I recently married is Swedish and *the* reason I moved to Sweden. That would have made it the craziest story though, wouldn't it have?"

"Absolutely."

"Anyways, Erin's younger sister Kira, the very day they found the bottle, wrote me back a note—a new letter, sealed in a different bottle. It was tossed into Donegal Bay at the very spot they found my Canadian Pepsi bottle."

"It would have been cool if Kira's bottle was found too eh?" I mention as I finish the last of my now cold pizza.

"It was."

"What?"

"Yup."

"Where?"

"In Scotland. Took one year to be found."

"Let me get this straight. Of the six bottles thrown into the water in your story. . . two from you, two from your cousin, one from the lady in Quebec and the one from Kira . . . *three* were actually recovered?"

"Yup. Perhaps the other ones will too someday!"

"Three for six. 500. Not a bad average."

With our lunch break coming to an end, our bill paid, we climb the steps to our waiting vehicle. I duck my head climbing into the passenger seat of the small European car, shaking my head in disbelief at the amazing story I just heard.

"Anything is possible," Philippe nods as his hand thrusts the manual transmission into gear.

I think he's right.

Svenska Kocken
(Swedish Chef)

"A great attitude does much more than turn on the lights in our worlds; it seems to magically connect us to all sorts of serendipitous opportunities that were somehow absent before the change."

—Earl Nightingale

When most Canadians think of Sweden they see a country of beautiful, blue-eyed blondes, dream of bargains on IKEA furniture, hum ABBA tunes, reflect on past hockey glory, or discuss who should win the next Nobel Peace Prize. Not me. Sweden is forever linked with a childhood love: a television character who made me laugh hysterically. Little did I know that a day would come when my favorite Muppet character would hold out his human hand and greet me, "There you are!"

I toured Sweden on an MLB Envoy assignment, and on the second week of my trip I traveled to Rättvik on the shores of Lake Siljan. Swedish for *right bay*, Rättvik had just over 11,000 residents, all apparently with a fondness for red as most dwellings had been painted in *Falun Röd*, the color of dried blood. The buildings dotted the landscape like blanched barns and I found it interesting that many houses had siding that ran vertically as opposed to the normal horizontal back home.

This logo was developed by Philippe Longchamps and is a bit softer in tone than the original one.

The home field of the local baseball club was situated in a small valley where a small butcher shop was once located. That sanguinary heritage had also been honored in the team's name—*The Rättvik Butchers Baseboll Klubb*—and its original logo included a bloody silver cleaver. As Envoy to the Butchers, my schedule included a *baseboll skola* each morning, afternoon practices with their youth programs and evening sessions with the adult team. I was still recovering from shoulder surgery and had to throw left-handed the first part of the trip. Moving the L screen and throwing at close range certainly improved my accuracy. In the beginning anything beyond fifty feet was anyone's guess where the ball would go.

I initially couldn't see the ball diamond from the parking lot when I first arrived there. Upon further inspection I was pleased to see that the field itself was carved out some 100-150 feet down from the road. It was in great shape and had a pleasant hitting background of tall trees that lined the length of the backstop, home base side, and the entire out-field fence. I was reminded that I was indeed in a foreign land when I looked up from the oversized dugouts and saw *BORTA* and *HEMMA* posted where VISITORS and HOME would have been back in North America.

On the first day of the *skola*, I arrived early and headed for the storage room. Feet scuffled outside and I heard the chatter of high-pitched voices as I laid out bats, balls and gloves (*handskens*). The participants in the morning session had

It is always neat to see Visitors and Home in a foreign language on ballpark scoreboards around the world.

begun to arrive. I caught my first glimpse as I peering out of the storage shed and seeing them spill into the dugout. Kids. If there was one of them who approached nine years old then he would have been the grandpa of the bunch. This truly was an unusual introductory *skola*—a camp for youngsters who were green horns—most had never even heard of baseball, let alone seen it played.

"Good morning! My name is Brent Loehr and I will be working with you this week helping you learn more about the great game of baseball." Silence. Blank stares. I paused and waited for a translator to make sense of my English. The kids scattered along the dugout bench sat listless and the adults who stood off to the side smoking looked perplexed. I tried again with a shorter sentence. Nothing. Apparently, the interpreter who was supposed to be there for the start of the session had not arrived yet.

I scanned the parents and kids who had looked back at me with complete bewilderment. "Hmm. At this rate I had better work on my Swedish." I launched into a spiel of improvised, mock-Swedish—a string of gobbledygook—that was wrapped up with "Bjork, bjork, bjork!" I did my best not to giggle when the small crowd of adults roared with laughter at my spot-on impression of my favorite character from the *Muppet Show*—the Swedish Chef. The fledgling players were steadfast in their silence.

As the eruption of the parents subsided, I heard P.G. Sjoberg, my host and club contact, blurt behind me to another adult, "Ha! Kuprik!"

I turned to look at him. "What?"

"Kuprik. The Chef. He's from Rättvik you know."

"The Swedish Chef?"

"Yes."

P.G. was a character: funny mannerisms, witty charm, busy-bee nature and liked by all. His receded, frizzy, salt-and-pepper hair flowed onto his shoulders and his thick mustache made me think he was more Italian than Swedish. I felt that his statement about *"The Chef"* was as likely as the tooth fairy coming out of the dugout and swinging a bat in the on-deck circle, waiting for her chance to hit one out of the park. There had been no time to discuss P.G.'s banter—a bunch of kids, under ten, called for my full attention. Envoy work varies and often was geared towards developing elite athletes. This was the polar opposite. Fortunately, it was not the first time I had put on a clinic for beginners. I dug deep into my bag of tricks and explained the complexities of balls and strikes, walks and strikeouts, fair balls and foul balls to this crew of non-English-speaking baseball rookies. When we taught base running we actually used miniature soccer balls and played a version of what Westerners might know as kick ball from their days in P. E. It was very controlled and a good way to introduce foul lines, base paths, running through first and the like.

Anytime P.G. and I were together our game of "Q and A" began. We both wanted to learn as much as we could about the other's culture—and get in a few good licks of teasing along the way. The drive from the ballpark after the morning session was no exception.

"You are rare you know," P.G. said.

"Why is that?"

"You like *Kalles.*"

"Like it . . . I love it!" Delectable *Kalles* caviar came in a blue toothpaste-like tube, ready to grace whatever it was lucky enough to be smeared on—usually *Leksandsbröd*, a form of dry, crisp bread with a consistency similar to a cracker.

P.G. changed the subject. "Your name, Loehr, is hard to pronounce."

"It rhymes with no hair." I pointed to my shaved head. "How can you think that is hard to say when *Sjoberg* is pronounced 'Weyberry' and P.G. sounds like 'Peh Geh'?

Apparently, P.G. was in a mood for non-sequiturs. "Forty thousand extra people will be in Rättvik during Week 31 you know."

"What is Week 31?"

"We count down the year by the week instead of referring to months. The first week in January is Week 1 . . . the last week of the year is Week 52. Christmas is during Week 51."

"Makes sense. Why the extra 40,000 people?"

"Classic Car Week. You will see. It will occur the week you come back from your assignment at Skovda and Lithuania. People from across Europe will cruise classic cars, camp, and celebrate all week long. The local radio station plays nothing but 50s and 60s American-style music that week."

"Neat."

We turned off the main drag and drove up a steep hill. P.G.'s son, Kristoffer, worked on the lift at the *Rättvik Slalombacke och Sommarrodel*—a summer ski hill where customers, seated in a chair, descended on a bobsleigh-like trail and wound their way to the bottom. A consummate performer, Kristoffer juggled anything and everything from knives to baseball bats and even breathed fire (I would stroke fire breathing off my bucket list when I scorched the midday sky with flames, under his careful instruction, a few days later).

"See that building?" P.G. pointed to the top of the slope. "Kuprik filmed a television show for the Discovery Channel there last Thursday."

"Kuprik?"

"The Chef. The one I spoke of. The *Svenska Kocken*—the Swedish Chef you imitated," he said with a mischievous smile.

I had encountered some silly things during my trips overseas, so prior to leaving Canada for Sweden, I was not surprised when someone back home had asked what oddity I expected to encounter in Sweden. I had casually replied, "The Swedish Chef of course . . . and I'll get him to make me dinner to boot." Obviously this was said in jest as the Swedish Chef was as real to me then as the Easter Bunny.

At the lift area that overlooked Lake Siljan we met up with a friend of P.G.'s named Filip Hagberg. It didn't take long before P.G. told him about my fascination with The Swedish Chef.

"You would like to speak with him," Filip said. "I give him a call."

P.G.'s chum whipped out his cell phone and punched in some numbers. "Kuprik?" I waited as he continued in Swedish.

"He wants to talk with you," Filip said as he handed over the phone.

A familiar voice rang in my ear—like a hammed imitation of the Muppet Swedish Chef.

"Seriously though," the voice said in very good English, "this is Lars. Lars Backman. People call me Kuprik. I am the Chef. Well, actually I am me, but the Chef is me too I guess." It was obvious that Lars had spent time in the United States. He spoke in unblemished English. "What are you doing tomorrow?" he asked as though he had just been reunited with a long lost friend. "My catering business is putting out a spread in a nearby town. Think you can make it for lunch? I always have room at my table for American friends."

That night, I returned to the Sjoberg home for an amazing dinner cooked by another type of Swedish chef—P.G.'s wife Lena. Who knew there were so many varieties of pickled fish? One thing about Sweden, though. The coffee jumped up, strangled, and then beat you with its jet-black strength. I forced down each sip. Chewed coffee beans would have tasted weaker.

"I think I will have something to talk about now when I get called for that radio interview," I said.

"What are you talking about?" asked P.G.'s daughter Carolina.

"When I was in Stockholm I was called by the CBC back home for an interview. They wanted to know how the trip was going, what Sweden was like, and if anything interesting happened so far. I told them to give me a couple of weeks."

"Why would meeting a cook be news?" she asked.

"A cook! We're talking about The Swedish Chef!

I explained that the Swedish Chef—my favorite Jim Henson character of all-time—was the one I waited for with utmost anticipation on the Muppet Show. Each of The Chef's vignettes showcased a different culinary folly unfolding in a makeshift kitchen. The opening scene of his skit always showed him dancing along, singing in mock-Swedish, waving his cooking utensils to the beat. At the end of the intro the Chef would toss his equipment haphazardly into the air behind him while he sang his signature ending "Bjork, bjork, bjork."

YouTube was in its infancy, untroubled by the niceties of copyright, so umpteen compilations of the Swedish Chef's finest moments were still available online. I added a clip to my travel blog. The Sjoberg family watched as the Muppet Chef spoke gibberish and put on a slapstick display of cooking incompetence, using unorthodox methods to create common dishes blended with clever (or not so clever) puns. We watched as the Chef shot a hole through a bun with a shotgun (his "boom-boom") to make a donut, served "meat balls" to his audience with a tennis racquet, spread chocolate on an antlered puppet to pass for "chocolate moose," and put ground beef into a shoe to make "meat loafers." The Sjobergs' laughed when I told them The Swedish Chef's saga should have been in their school curriculum (perhaps drilled in hypnotically with Abba music in the background). I am a child at heart and the kid in me certainly does come out—especially when I exaggerate.

A collection of older kids had sessions as well as an adult team in the evening. The latter was focused on what they called 'tricks': planned pick-off plays for the most part. They were also interested in how far I could hit or throw a baseball. Apparently a fellow there was related to someone from Sweden who had held the Guinness World Record for throwing a golf ball. Goodness. My shoulder cringed at the thought.

Happily, there was a gap in my schedule the next afternoon as there was something else booked for the youth. I had an unusually long break at midday when the afternoon sessions would have normally been sandwiched. Vikarbyn, where Lars Backman cooked that day, was about *one Swedish mile* from Rättvik. Sweden uses the metric system, but *a Swedish mile* was a common reference and denoted the distance of ten kilometers. My hometown of Muenster, Saskatchewan seemed like a hop, skip and a jump from Saskatoon at eleven Swedish miles versus labeling the journey at 110 kilometers. Perhaps this euphemism allowed Swedes to believe that they drove shorter distances, at less cost: gasoline there was over double the price we paid in Canada that summer.

It was market day in Vikarbyn. Through the car window I saw a smorgasbord of wares: old books discarded from store shelves, fresh strawberries, mono-colored clothes, and handmade crafts that included the symbol of the area—a Dolla Hast—a handheld wooden statue of a doll horse, painted fire engine red.

P.G. dropped me off and parked the vehicle while I walked around and explored. The vibe on that warm summer day reminded me of a radio station live on location. I had come upon a new model white van—fifteen- passenger style. It had a wide yellow stripe banded around it that was outlined on the top and bottom in equally fat lines of light blue—the flag colors of Sweden. Towards the back of the van a caricature of a chef was painted with the bold yellow caption *KUPRIK— Svenska Kocken.* I had repeatedly rehearsed this phrase the other night at supper, "Svenska Kocken . . . Swedish Cook." I had hoped to impress Lars Backman with this and other Swedish phrases I had learned so far.

A crowd had gathered around a canopy tent, dark blue, with professional looking company logos printed on its canvas walls. Picnic tables were plentiful and offered a spot for relaxation as people visited and nibbled on food to the sound of upbeat, yet gentle, background music. A long line of people of all ages had already formed and their smiling faces and cheery demeanor gave me the impression that they were waiting for something everyone else *needed*.

I brought out my video camera and captured the moment. I panned the scene and felt like a visitor to a zoo attempting to view a favorite exotic animal without disturbing its day-to-day behavior. I saw Kuprik through my lens. Dressed like a stereotypical chef, he wore a double-breasted white shirt and pants, chef's puffy hat and dark blue apron. A handkerchief, in Swedish colors, was tied loosely around his neck with class. It appeared that he had sampled a bit of his own cooking over the years, yet still had bounce in his step that was a youthful contrast to the grayed hair, dusted with red, that he wore so well.

As I zoomed in, I saw more clearly that the Swedish Chef truly enjoyed the moment as he bobbed his head and hummed with his eyes closed occasionally. His lips pursed in a singing motion as he casually interacted with customers. It took a few moments to realize that he wore something his puppet version did not—a set of small, stylish glasses, and that he and his staff prepared the meal in woks.

P.G. had taken the opportunity to sneak around to the cooking area and let the Chef know I was there. The next thing I knew, Lars "Kuprik" Backman bounded towards me, hand outstretched, "There you are!"

P.G. grabbed my video camera and, documentary style, filmed this collision of fact and fiction. Backman must have had absolute faith in his workers as we chatted off to the side for about ten minutes. He explained that as a youngster, growing up in Sweden, he had been surrounded by cooking and the culinary industry. In 1968, he left for the United States to help a friend at a Swedish style restaurant in California, the Viking Horn, and ended up working on the outskirts of Beverly Hills. He quickly moved up the cooking ladder to become head chef at the largest Holiday Inn in the area.

One of the Chefmobiles used by the one and only Lars 'Kuprik' Backman.

Backman recalled the time he was invited to do a cooking segment on a popular daily show, *Tempo Tempo*, a forerunner to *Good Morning America*. He was told he was supposed to present Swedish cooking with the help of their host, a young Regis Philbin. What he didn't know—the show was filmed live. When the crew began to count down "5, 4, 3, 2 . . .

you're on!" he had stood dumbfounded. Neither English nor Swedish had come out of his mouth, rather a form of gibberish, as he nervously fumbled, sweating profusely.

The television spot was a comedy of errors and even though the live audience was heartily amused, Lars said that at the time he was traumatized. He would eventually recover and make his way into the film industry, taking on the role of Master Chef for 20th Century Fox—preparing meals for the cast and crew of some of the biggest films and television shows in production: *M*A*S*H*, *Starsky and Hutch*, *Dynasty*, and the *Love Boat.* Apparently, Jim Henson, creator of the *Muppet Show*, had seen footage of the Chef's cooking debacle on television, and a new character emerged—The Swedish Chef.

"I originally planned to stay in California for six months, but fifteen years soon passed and I had still hung my hat in Hollywood," Backman said. After his mother fell ill, he eventually returned home to Sweden to be closer to his family and continued on with his career in the cooking industry.

"Where are you from again?" he asked.

"Saskatchewan . . . Canada."

"Hmm," he said, eyebrows raised, uncertain of where that was.

"Between Edmonton and Winnipeg," I said.

In Sweden I was usually able to clue the location of my home due to the popularity of the National Hockey League's Edmonton Oilers and Winnipeg Jets franchises.

Lars 'Kuprik' Backman and I could have talked the day away. It was as though I had found a long-lost uncle.

"I loved the Swedish Chef and had no idea that there was an actual person who inspired it," I confessed as we snapped a few pictures near his catering van. As our meeting drew to a close he said, "Your money is no good here. Sit down and I will bring you dinner."

The cook later hand-delivered a scrumptious meal: lightly-browned chicken breast, yellow-sauced rice and stir-fry vegetables that included carrots, potatoes, broccoli and cauliflower. The aroma permeated the air and invited multiple inhalations as it brought pleasure to my nostrils. A small salad, with a unique sweet and sour flavor, complimented the delectable smorg.

After P.G. and I finished eating we thanked the Chef for his time. "How long are you here for?" he asked.

"I am gone at the end of the week but I will be back for Week 31."

"Ah, Classic Car Week. You will enjoy that! I will have my catering business there at the city-center. Stop by for a visit and we'll chat. Maybe I can pick you up tomorrow from the ballpark, take you to my house, and show you some of my memorabilia from the movie years?"

"Deal. Hey, it was an honor and pleasure to meet the real *Svenska Kuken*," I said as I snuck in the phrase I had practiced the night before. We shook hands.

I repeatedly thanked P.G. for making the trip that afternoon possible as we drove off to the park. For some reason he could not control his laughter and was barely able to breathe.

"Why are you laughing?"

"You!"

"What?"

"You did not call him the *Svenska Kocken* like you wanted to." P.G. sputtered between gasps. "You said *Kuken*. You meant to say Swedish Cook . . . but you said Swedish *Cock*!"

When the CBC interviewed me the next day, my date with the cook was a big part of what I told them about, as was baseball, and interestingly enough, gas prices. I conveniently neglected to mention my limited mastery of the Swedish language and my slip-up calling him something quite different than what I had planned. Later, while on the internet, I came across an interview of Jerry Juhl—a Muppet Show *writer. It had been given four years prior to my meeting with the Chef. In it, Juhl claimed unequivocally that the character of the Swedish Chef had been created with no inspiration other than his and Jim Henson (who died in 1990). Mr. Backman told me, on my visit during Classic Car week, that he had heard the Juhl statement. In Kuprik's view, the "powers that be" refused to acknowledge that his actions had inspired the creation of The Swedish Chef character as royalties may have then been required. It was a dead issue to him and not worth pursuing.*

Upon researching background material for this story I discovered that Jerry Juhl had now also passed away . . . two months after I met the Chef for the first time. Regardless, Kuprik will always be "The Chef" to me. The only thing that really made me wonder about him was that he said he, "was invited all the time to attend professional baseball games" when he lived in the states, but that he "couldn't be bothered to watch such a boring sport." Perhaps he should indeed stick to cooking.

If You Build It . . .

"Vision without action is merely a dream. Action without vision just passes the time. Vision with action can change the world."

—Joel Barker

My favorite baseball movie of all-time is Field of Dreams. *An element of pride exists for me in that the screenplay was adapted from a novel written by a man from Western Canada: William Patrick (W.P.) Kinsella. His work has always surrounded me and was an inspiration in my youth—especially given my passion for baseball and literature. The novel Bill Kinsella wrote,* Shoeless Joe, *on which* Field of Dreams *is based, was originally a short story called* "Shoeless Joe Jackson Goes to Iowa." *While collecting his writings, over time I discovered that nestled in with his baseball stories are pieces written about characters based on fictional First Nations reserves in Canada. Kinsella was criticized for his take on something he never lived through, to which he retorted about fiction writing, "You don't have to commit suicide to write about it . . . you only have to make it believable."*

Canadian author Bill Kinsella, a legend in terms of baseball writing.

Of the schools in the Midwestern United States that recruited me to play college baseball, one in Iowa fascinated me the most. The state had a romanticized pull on me as a parcel of land there was the set for the ball field used in *Field of Dreams*. One of the coaches from an Iowa university that had contacted me had been an extra in that movie—cast as one of the ghost ball players. I was intrigued when I read about it in a baseball program guide that was mailed out. Looking back, what a superficial reason to consider for attending a school.

After contemplating half a dozen offers I ended up accepting one from the University of North Dakota-Williston. Soon into my first semester there, an English prof named Lee Kruger, who had ties to Iowa, recognized my interest in writing and love of baseball. One day he showed up to class and set a book on my desk—a copy of a Kinsella book that I hadn't read yet: *Box Socials*. This was about the same time that another of W.P.'s works was made into a feature film called *Dance Me Outside*. That very same week I came across an anthology edition of *Spitball*, a literary baseball magazine, that contained an interview with W.P. Kinsella. I kept adding and adding his work to my collection that has been a part of my life ever since high school. In 2001, the James Horner score from *Field of Dreams* was the background music at my wedding.

When I watched the movie yet again after my dad died after a sudden illness, the film took on greater meaning for me. Not too many movies have brought tears to my eyes. Years later, after submitting an assignment that included Kinsella for a writing class at St. Peter's College, I was urged by instructor Allan Safarik, "You need to contact Bill. I know him actually. You need to chat with him about writing. Baseball writing in particular." Allan knew the writer from his time when he lived in British Columbia. I put out a request through Kinsella's agent and was thrilled when Bill himself emailed me back. We exchanged a few communications and he offered some advice. I always thought *I have to write something on him sometime.*

In January that very year, J.D. Salinger, whom Kinsella used as a character in *Shoeless Joe*, died at 91. A few years after that, when I knew my writings were going to be put into this collection, I contacted Bill Kinsella again, this time for an interview to be included in the upcoming release. He obliged. The more I read and learned about Kinsella the more enamored I became with his honest views on baseball, writing, and the publishing industry as a whole. I have always wanted to ask him some questions on the spellbinding evolution of his art, and finally got a chance:

When did your fascination with baseball begin?
Kinsella:
The only baseball we got was newspaper and we'd get the World Series on the radio. I remember the 1946 World Series—Boston and St. Louis. I was always fascinated by baseball even though I had never played it. My dad had played some minor league ball and we

always had some kind of Class C team or something in Edmonton and we watched baseball there fairly often.

What do you think it is about baseball that makes people so passionate about it?

Kinsella:

I think it is the open-endedness of the game that makes it so interesting. There is no limit on the imagination, everything else is enclosed by time limits and playing boundaries. The foul lines on a baseball field diverge forever and the possibilities are simply endless. That is what makes the game more fascinating than others.

I have read about your disdain of the writing establishment and of the sometimes cruel rejection letters you received early on in your career. Did you ever contemplate stopping writing? For "Shoeless Joe Jackson Goes to Iowa" in particular, was there ever a point in time where that story may not have been finished or written at all?

Kinsella:

No. I always knew I was good. It was the editors who didn't know what they were doing. (laughs). You have to believe that what you are doing is good even if it isn't. So I always knew that I was doing good stuff . . . it was just a matter of time until it was recognized. Eventually it was.

Can you tell me about the writing process for Shoeless Joe?

Kinsella:

I don't want to know where a story is going. If I know where it's going I'm bored with it already. I like to be surprised. I look for a good opening. A good opening line that draws the reader in and after that I keep saying, 'What if? What if? What if.' I still write a first draft in long hand and then I put it on the computer and then it is pretty well finished. I hate editing. In the old days it was the same except I would put it on the typewriter.

I am always intrigued by why writers choose the character names that they do. Did you consciously hunt for a tie-in of your surname 'Kinsella' with Salinger's work . . . if so, how did you stumble on it?

Kinsella:

When I decided I was going to use Salinger I read all of his collected and uncollected material. I reread 'Catcher' and I reread the nine stories and stumbled on several uncollected ones. I discovered that he had used Kinsella as a name twice in his works, so I thought, wow, hey there is the tie-in. My character can be Ray Kinsella and he can turn up on Salinger's door step and say, "Hey I am one of your fictional characters come to life."

How did you come across the amazing real-life character of Moonlight Graham?

Kinsella:

It was an accident. My father-in-law gave me a Baseball Encyclopedia for Christmas and I was leafing through it and I saw the name and I thought: Moonlight Graham . . . what a wonderful name. Who was this guy? After I saw that he had played one inning of baseball . . . wondered how he became "Moonlight" and since I was looking at ways to expand my story I thought that would be a way. He turned out to be a much more wonderful character in real life than anything I could have invented.

Can you tell me about Chisolm, Minnesota . . . the community Moonlight lived for decades once he left baseball?
Kinsella:

We went to Chisolm and I think that was the most wonderful thing about the whole process of writing the book. We walked into the Chisolm newspaper office and I told them who I was and what I was doing. I asked if they knew where I could get a picture of him and the lady turned around and parted the ferns on her filing cabinet and there was a picture of Doc Graham in his New York Giants uniform. I said I would give her "what money I had and my wristwatch while I go and take it to a photographer to get it copied as I know you value it." She was very nice. She let me take it downtown and get it copied.

Was there any role in your own relationship with your father when writing the story or is that implied author syndrome?
Kinsella:

(pauses) No, I don't think so. That was an add-on actually. I had finished the story and had just gone to Calgary to teach and my then girlfriend came up to visit me and she could type 200 words a minute or something and she was going to type the final version of the story for me and I stopped her at one point and asked, "How far along are you on the story . . . I just thought of something I would like to add to the end." She wasn't quite finished so that is where I added the business about the father. It was a touch I really added when it was all but finished really. It tied in perfectly though. The opening line is 'My father said he saw him years later' . . .and it certainly ties in with the end.

Did you ever think that when you wrote that short story years ago that it would develop into a novel?

Kinsella:

I didn't think it at the time. It was later suggested by a young editor at Houghton Mifflin who had not actually read the story but a review of the anthology in Publishers Weekly. *He wrote me and said, "If it's a novel we want to see it . . . and if it isn't it should be." I had never written a novel but I had written four books of short stories so I thought I don't see why I couldn't. I started working on it immediately.*

Can you tell me about the background of the book becoming a movie?

Kinsella:

The book came out in '82 and was immediately optioned by a small company and they held it for two years before it lapsed. I believe it was '84 when it was optioned and they hired someone to write the screenplay. I had just moved to B.C. I didn't pay any attention to it as 99 out of a 100 options lapse . . . all you do is enjoy the option money. Phil Robinson was really in love with the book and he phoned me and he sort of apologized for what he had to do knowing he couldn't get a 300 and some page novel into an hour and 20 minute movie. He said he would have to cut characters, have to telescope time, etc. I said to him it was as if I was a baker who baked a loaf of bread . . . you paid the proper price for the bread I don't care whether you feed it to your gerbils or make it into crustless sandwiches. It's your project. I don't understand people who are proprietary about their work. As long as I am paid properly I don't care what they do with it. They can make it into

The location of the movie site for the iconic Field of Dreams is intact at the former Lansing farm near Dyersville, Iowa.

a zombie movie if they want to. Phil took the finished screenplay to Paramount. They passed and Phil asked to take it elsewhere and he took it to one of the Gordon brothers and they took it to Universal and then they decided to make it.

What role did you have during the film? Any input or consulting?

Kinsella:

No. And I didn't want to. I know nothing about making movies, I know nothing about screenwriting. I am always appalled when I see a writer doing the screenplay for their work because they are such different mediums. Screenwriting is a collaborative effort and I work alone. I don't collaborate with anybody.

Were you asked at all about the casting of actors for the movie?

Kinsella:

No. I didn't even know who Kevin Costner was. They said they were going to cast him so I rented No Way Out *or something and I thought this guy is really good. Amy Madigan looked the part and I was really happy when they got James Earl Jones.*

Can you tell me about the context of where you saw the movie for the first time? Were you at an advance screening?

Kinsella:

No, I saw the finished product in the theater.

Have you been to the movie set in Iowa since for any kind of functions?

Kinsella:

Yes, I have been back a couple of times. I don't travel anymore . . . I'm getting old. I have been there three or four times though.

I understand that the movie set has taken a little bit of a life of its own now as even more of a tourist attraction?

Kinsella:

Yes. The Lansings sold out a year or two ago and I think Wade Boggs is involved and I don't know exactly what they are doing with it. The whole idea in the book was that it was for people to come to. No one would think even a little bit about paying $10 to come and run around the bases.

I read that you were struck as pedestrian by a vehicle in a serious accident. Did you really not write for years?

Kinsella:

That was overplayed in the press a lot. I had a concussion for about a year and I didn't do much of anything, but after that I kept writing.

It sort of coincided with the time that the publishing industry fell apart. See, I am one of the writers that's been totally passed by with that. I could never play with the big dogs but I was a successful midlist author. Midlist authors are gone now. You either go big or you go with the small presses. My hiatus coincided with the falling apart of the publishing industry.

When did it first hit you that your work has impacted so many in a positive way and what are your thoughts on its legacy?

Kinsella:

When Shoeless Joe came out I started to get letters by the 100s . . . then the 1000s, so I knew that I had hit something. I was in the right place at the right time. The short story was pretty much out of fashion and then from the mid-70s until about 1990 there was a resurgence of the short story. I was very lucky with my short fiction where you could publish a collection of short stories and if they were good you could sell a ton.

I greatly appreciate having the opportunity to interview you. I am indeed a fan and have an extensive collection of your works. It was an honor to have your ear again.

Kinsella:

Well, thank you very much. Bye now.

*   *   *

W.P. Kinsella penned a short story that eventually became a novel. That book was later adapted into a screenplay and made into a feature film nominated for three Academy Awards grossing tens of millions of dollars. The movie set still stands and has had over a million visitors; in fact, news stories report that a group called *Go the Distance Baseball LLC* purchased the 193-acre site and plan to create a tournament complex called "All-Star Ballpark Heaven." The asking price was $5.4 million dollars. The economic injection and job creation for the Dyersville area could be staggering.

Kinsella's vision was the genesis, and the words he put on paper and struck keystroke by keystroke on a typewriter, put into motion this creative evolution of art. It is impossible to measure the full impact of this legendary work; it will continue for generations. W.P. Kinsella exudes confidence . . . but what if his short story had never been published? What if?

CPSIA information can be obtained at www.ICGtesting.com
Printed in the USA
LVOW10s0047160715

446361LV00001B/51/P

9 781938 545627